Process Management Excellence

Excellence

The Art of Excelling
in Process Management

Process Management Excellence

The Art of Excelling in Process Management

Book 1 in the five-part series
The Five Pillars of Organizational Excellence

H. James Harrington, Ph.D.

Foreword by Dr. Armand V. Feigenbaum

Paton Press LLC
Chico, California

Most Paton Press books are available at quantity discounts when purchased in bulk.
For more information, contact:

Paton Press LLC
P.O. Box 44
Chico, CA 95927-0044
Telephone: 1-888-377-5480
Fax: (530) 342-5471
E-mail: *books@patonpress.com*
Web: *www.patonpress.com*

Printed in the United States of America

10 09 08 07 06   5 4 3 2 1

ISBN-13: 978-1-932828-06-1
ISBN-10: 1-932828-06-0

Library of Congress Cataloging-in-Publication Data
Harrington, H. J. (H. James)
 Process management excellence: the art of excelling in process management / by H. James Harrington.
     p. cm. — (Five pillars of organizational excellence; 1)
  ISBN 1-932828-06-0
 1. Industrial management. 2. Organizational effectiveness. 3. Organizational change. I. Title.
  HD31.H34537 2006
  658.4'013--dc22
                            2005030025

Notice of Liability
The information in this book is distributed on an "as is" basis, without warranty. Although every precaution has been taken in the preparation of the book, neither the author nor Paton Press LLC shall have any liability to any person or entity with respect to any loss or damage caused or alleged to be caused directly or indirectly by the information contained in this book.

Staff
Publisher: Scott M. Paton
Editor: Finn Kraemer
Book design: David Hurst

CONTENTS

ABOUT THE AUTHOR

In the book *Tech Trending* (Capstone, 2001) by Amy Zuckerman, H. James Harrington was referred to as "the quintessential tech trender." *The New York Times* referred to him as having a ". . . knack for synthesis and an open mind about packaging his knowledge and experience in new ways—characteristics that may matter more as prerequisites for new-economy success than technical wizardry . . . "

H. James Harrington, Ph.D.
CEO, Harrington Institute Inc.

Present Responsibilities

Harrington now serves as the chief executive officer for the Harrington Institute. He also serves as the chairman of the board for a number of businesses and as the U.S. chairman of Technologies for Project Management at the University of Quebec.

Harrington is recognized as one of the world leaders in applying performance improvement methodologies to business processes.

Previous Experience

In February 2002, Harrington retired as the COO of Systemcorp ALG, a leading supplier of knowledge management and project management software solutions. Prior to this, he served as a principal and one of the leaders in the Process Innovation Group at Ernst & Young. He was with IBM for more than thirty years as a senior engineer and project manager.

Harrington is past chairman of the prestigious International Academy for Quality and past president of the American Society for Quality. He is also an active member of the Global Knowledge Economics Council.

Credentials

The Harrington/Ishikawa Medal, presented yearly by the Asia Pacific Quality Organization, was named after Harrington to recognize his many contributions to the region. In 1997, the Quebec Society for Quality named their quality award "The Harrington/Neron Medal," honoring Harrington for his many contributions to Canada's quality movement. In 2000, the Sri Lanka national quality award was named after him.

Harrington's contributions to performance improvement around the world have brought him many honors and awards, including the Edwards Medal, the Lancaster Medal, ASQ's Distinguished Service Medal, China's Magnolia Award, and many others. He was appointed the honorary advisor to the China Quality Control Association, and he was elected to the Singapore Productivity Hall of Fame in 1990. He has been named lifetime honorary president of the Asia Pacific Quality Organization and honorary director of the Chilean Association of Quality Control.

Harrington has been elected a Fellow of the British Quality Control Organization and the American Society for Quality. He was also elected an honorary member of the quality societies in Taiwan, Argentina, Brazil, Colombia, and Singapore. He is listed in *Who's Who Worldwide* and *Men of Distinction Worldwide*. He has presented hundreds of papers on performance improvement and organizational management structure at local, state, national, and international levels.

Harrington is a prolific author, having published hundreds of technical reports and magazine articles. He has authored twenty-eight books and ten software packages.

Other books by H. James Harrington

- *The Improvement Process* (McGraw-Hill, 1987, a best-selling business book that year)
- *Poor-Quality Cost* (Marcel Dekker, 1987)
- *Excellence—The IBM Way* (American Society for Quality, 1988)
- *The Quality/Profit Connection* (American Society for Quality, 1988)
- *Business Process Improvement* (McGraw-Hill, 1991, the first book about process redesign)
- *The Mouse Story* (Ernst & Young, 1991)
- *Of Tails and Teams* (American Society for Quality, 1994)
- *Total Improvement Management* (McGraw-Hill, 1995)
- *High Performance Benchmarking* (McGraw-Hill, 1996)
- *The Complete Benchmarking Implementation Guide* (McGraw-Hill, 1996)
- *ISO 9000 and Beyond* (McGraw-Hill, 1996)
- *The Business Process Improvement Workbook* (McGraw-Hill, 1997)
- *The Creativity Toolkit—Provoking Creativity in Individuals and Organizations* (McGraw-Hill, 1998)
- *Statistical Analysis Simplified—The Easy-to-Understand Guide to SPC and Data Analysis* (McGraw-Hill, 1998)
- *Area Activity Analysis—Aligning Work Activities and Measurements to Enhance Business Performance* (McGraw-Hill, 1998)
- *Reliability Simplified—Going Beyond Quality to Keep Customers for Life* (McGraw-Hill, 1999)
- *ISO 14000 Implementation—Upgrading Your EMS Effectively* (McGraw-Hill, 1999)
- *Performance Improvement Methods—Fighting the War on Waste* (with Kenneth C. Lomax, McGraw-Hill, 1999)
- *Simulation Modeling Methods—An Interactive Guide to Results-Based Decision Making* (McGraw-Hill, 2000)
- *Project Change Management—Applying Change Management to Improvement Projects* (with Daryl R. Conner and Nicholas L. Horney, McGraw-Hill, 2000)
- *E-Business Project Manager* (American Society for Quality, 2002)
- *Project Management Excellence: The Art of Excelling in Process Management* (Paton Press, 2006)
- *Change Management Excellence: The Art of Excelling in Change Management* (Paton Press, 2006)
- *Knowledge Management Excellence: The Art of Excelling in Knowledge Management* (Paton Press, 2006)
- *Resource Management Excellence: The Art of Excelling in Resource Management* (Paton Press, 2006)
- *Making Teams Hum* (Paton Press, 2006)

DEDICATION

I dedicate this book to the many friends I have worked with through the years at the American Society for Quality and the International Academy for Quality. Without their free and open sharing of best practices, I would not have been able to write this book. I will never stop learning from them.

ACKNOWLEDGMENTS

I want to acknowledge Candy Rogers, who transcribed and edited endless hours of dictation into the finished product. I could not have done it without her help. To my friends at the American Society for Quality and the International Academy for Quality, I want to thank you for your many contributions to the concepts expressed in this book.

I also want to recognize the contributions made by the team from Harrington Institute Inc. But most of all, I want to recognize the contributions made by my wife, Marguerite. She's always there when I need her.

FOREWORD

Jim Harrington is one of those very rare business leaders who combines outstanding inherent ability, effective management skills, broad technology background and great effectiveness in producing results. His record of accomplishment is a very long, broad and deep one that is highly and favorably recognized.

Dr. Harrington also has a highly effective capacity for clearly explaining how he has been consistently applying these strengths to help produce outstanding business results. In this book, he brings together his business experience and his communications expertise to focus on how to achieve organizational excellence in today's brutally demanding, twenty-first century global environment.

It's a rapidly changing environment that's now creating a competitive situation in which nothing—certainly not organizational excellence—stands still in a world where the fast devour the slow, and where change is the single thing that remains constant. The only way in which companies can hold the momentum and visibility of their results in today's economic, social, and governmental climate is to extend them relentlessly.

Organizational excellence is correspondingly a major continuing work in progress and center point for accomplishing such outcomes today. This is both in the significant changes in how it's led successfully in companies as well as in terms of its "how to do" work content for men and women throughout all of their activities in the organization. How well we understand and are able to provide genuine, consistent, credible and results-apparent leadership to this will influence the competitive futures of our companies and of our own jobs.

It is, therefore, both timely and fortunate that Jim Harrington is providing this book to help as a guide in this demanding task of both fully understanding and in accelerating organizational excellence for the twenty-first century world.

The fundamental theme that is carried on throughout the book is that, for competitive leadership in today's environment where circumstances change constantly, you have to excel equally constantly. The book discusses in clear practical terms the key areas — i.e., the five pillars—for accomplishing the required organizational excellence. They are amplified by examples that help to make the book highly readable.

What sets the true corporate leaders apart from the followers is the consistency of their leadership emphasis for accomplishing such results of excellence, especially in times of business stress in which the fast and committed overwhelm the slow and the uncertain. The Five Pillars of Organizational Excellence series is sure to help in accomplishing this purpose.

—*Dr. Armand V. Feigenbaum*
CEO, General Systems Corp.

"Dr. Armand V. Feigenbaum is the world's foremost leader in developing and applying quality methodologies to improve organizational performance. If Walter Shewhart is the father of modern quality, Dr. Feigenbaum is his first son."

—*H. James Harrington*

PREFACE

"No person or company should be content to stay where they are, no matter how successful they now seem to be."

—Stephen R. Covey, Ph.D.
The Seven Habits of Highly Effective People

This series was written for a small group of organizations. It's not for traditionalists, the weak of heart, or for organizations that believe winning a national quality award is their ultimate objective. This series was written for organizations that aren't content to be anything less than the best they can be. It's for organizations that want to stand out from the crowd and that hunger to obtain optimum results in the five Ps:

- *Pride.* Employees are proud of their work and their organization.
- *Performance.* The entire organization operates at high levels of efficiency and effectiveness.
- *Profit.* The organization is profitable, able to pay its employees good salaries, and pay higher-than-average dividends to its investors.
- *Prestige.* The organization is considered an admirable place to work for and is known for its highly desired products and services.
- *Pleasure.* Employees enjoy coming to work because they are doing something worthwhile in a friendly, supportive environment.

Good is no longer good enough. Doing the right thing "right" is not good enough. Having the highest quality and being the most productive doesn't suffice today. To survive in today's competitive environment, you must excel. (See figure P.1.) To excel, an organization needs to focus on all parts of itself, optimizing the use and effectiveness of all of its resources. To excel, it must provide "knock their socks off" products and services. An organization must be so innovative and creative that its customers say, "I didn't know they could do that!"

After years of working with all types of organizations and using many different approaches to improve performance, I've come to realize that five key elements must be managed for an organization to excel. I call them the "five pillars of organizational excellence." All five must be managed creatively and simultaneously. Top management's job is to keep

> "To compete and win, we must redouble our efforts, not only in the quality of our goods and services, but in the quality of our thinking, in the quality of our response to our customers, in the quality of our decision making, in the quality of everything we do."
> —E. S. Woolard
> Chairman and CEO, Dupont

Figure P.1 Organizational Excellence

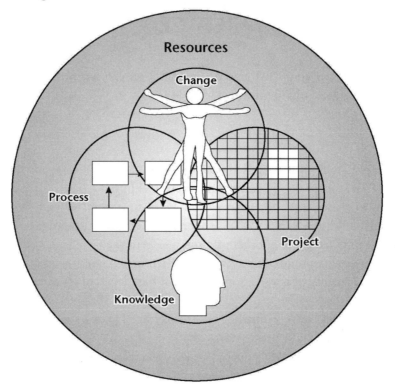

all these elements moving ahead simultaneously. To concentrate on one or two alone is a surefire formula for failure. Priorities might shift, causing an individual pillar to move from "very important" to simply "important," but it should never shift lower than that.

The processes discussed in this series are designed to permanently change an organization by skillfully managing its five key pillars. Each of these management pillars is not new by itself, but by combining and managing them together, a holistic approach to improving an organization's performance is possible. (See figure P.2.)

The five pillars of organizational excellence are:

■ *Process management excellence.* We must manage our processes and continuously improve them because they are the way we do business.

■ *Project management excellence.* We must manage our projects because they are the way we obtain major improvements in our processes.

■ *Change management excellence.* We must manage the organization so that it can cope with the chaos it will be subjected to by the magnitude and quantity of necessary changes.

■ *Knowledge management excellence.* We must manage the organization's knowledge, its most valuable asset. (Knowledge gives an organization its competitive advantage, as technology can easily be reverse-engineered and transferred to any place in the world almost overnight.)

■ *Resource management excellence.* We must manage our resources and assets because they are what drive our business results.

By effectively managing these five key pillars and leveraging their interdependencies and reactions, an organization can bring about a marvelous self-transformation. It will emerge from its restricting cocoon and float on the winds of success and self-fulfillment.

Organizational excellence is designed to permanently change an organization by focusing on the five pillars of excellence. Learning to manage the pillars together is the key to success in the endless pursuit of improved performance. To help you in this endeavor, each volume in this five-book series addresses one of the pillars. The series consists of the following books:

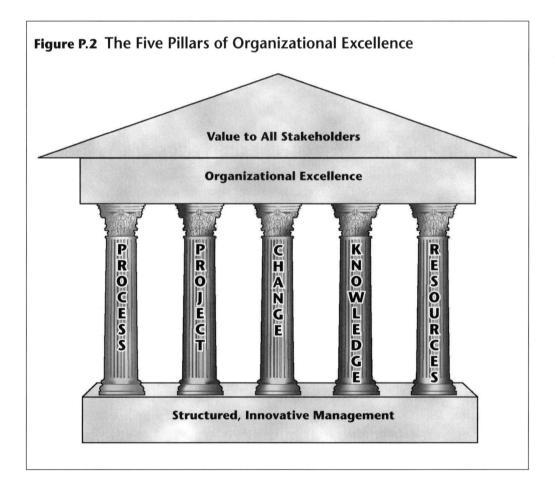

Figure P.2 The Five Pillars of Organizational Excellence

Value to All Stakeholders

Organizational Excellence

PROCESS PROJECT CHANGE KNOWLEDGE RESOURCES

Structured, Innovative Management

- *Process Management Excellence: The Art of Excelling in Process Management*
- *Project Management Excellence: The Art of Excelling in Project Management*
- *Change Management Excellence: The Art of Excelling in Change Management*
- *Knowledge Management Excellence: The Art of Excelling in Knowledge Management*
- *Resource Management Excellence: The Art of Excelling in Resource Management*

None of the five pillars can individually support organizational excellence. All of them must be present and equally strong to support the weight of success for all of its stakeholders. The challenge that excellent organizations face today is how to nurture an innovative learning culture while maintaining the procedures and structure to ensure optimum performance as well as customer and investor satisfaction. The Five Pillars of Organizational Excellence series was designed to help you solve this dilemma.

Because it's important to understand how the five pillars interact with and support each other, a short discussion about each of them follows.

PILLAR I—PROCESS MANAGEMENT EXCELLENCE

"Your processes manage the organization, not your managers."
—HJH

The process management concept certainly isn't new to management professionals; it's the basis of most improvement methodologies.

Definition: A *process* is a series of interconnected activities that takes input, adds value to it, and produces output. It's how organizations work their day-to-day routines. Your organization's processes define how it operates.

To manage a process, the following must be defined and agreed upon:
- An output requirement statement between process owners and customers
- An input requirement statement between process owners and suppliers
- A process that can transform suppliers' input into output that meets customers' performance and quality requirements

- Feedback measurement systems between process and customers, and between process and suppliers
- The method by which people are trained to understand the process
- A measurement system within the process

These six key factors should be addressed when designing a process. However, the problem facing most organizations is that many of their support processes were never designed in the first place. They were created in response to a need without understanding what a process is.

> **"Most individuals, teams, and groups within an organization will take the path of least resistance. Inevitably, over time, they will function at the lowest level of acceptability."**
> **—William J. Schwarz CEO, CEO Alliance and the Center for Inspired Performance**

The Two Approaches to Process Management

There are two basic approaches to managing processes:

- The micro-level approach, which is directed at managing processes within a natural work team or an individual department.
- The macro-level approach, which is directed at managing processes that flow across departments and/or functions within the organization.

Most of the work that quality professionals do involves continuously improving processes. Some of the tools they use include design of experiments, process capability studies, root cause analysis, document control, quality circles, suggestion systems, Six Sigma, Shewhart's cycles, ISO 9001, and just-in-time manufacturing and supplier qualification.

In excellent organizations, management requires each natural work team (or department) to continuously improve the processes it uses.

Refining a process is an ongoing activity. If the refinement process is working as it should, the total process's efficiency and effectiveness should be improving at a rate of 10 to 15 percent a year. In most cases, the project team focuses on the major problems that reflect across departments and reap such a harvest within three to twelve months. At that time, the project team can be disbanded and the process

> **"If you [management] create an expectation of continuous product or service improvement but fail to deliver on that expectation, you will see a buildup of fear and negative forecasting."**
> **—Stephen R. Covey, Ph.D.**
> ***The Seven Habits of Highly Effective People***

refinement activities turned over to the natural work teams involved in the process. Area activity analysis methodology, which is discussed later in this book, is the most effective approach to process refinement.

By focusing on its processes and working with its suppliers, IBM reported that, "Between 1997 and 2001, the hardware reliability of our high-end servers improved by more than 200 percent while computing power increased by a factor of four."

PILLAR II—PROJECT MANAGEMENT EXCELLENCE

"How can you compete when more than 70 percent of your improvement efforts are unsuccessful?"

—HJH

According to the "Chaos Report" compiled by the Standish Group International:

- Only 26 percent of all projects are successful.
- Forty percent of all information technology (IT) projects fail or are canceled.

Processes define how organizations function, and they are the means by which organizations improve other processes.

Definition: A *project* is a temporary endeavor undertaken to create a unique product or service.

There are endless examples of poor project management. Two current examples are:

- NASA's space station Freedom was originally budgeted for $8 billion; costs are now up to $32 billion and climbing.
- The 2004 Olympic Games held in Greece were 300 percent over budget one year prior to the opening.

Projects in most organizations are mission-critical activities, and delivering quality products on time is non-negotiable. Even for information technology (IT) projects, things have changed: Benchmark organizations are completing 90 percent of their projects within 10 percent of budget and schedule. Information systems organizations that establish standards for project management, including a project office, are cutting their major project cost overruns, delays, and cancellations by 50 percent.

Process redesign and process reengineering are two of the most important projects that organizations undertake. These types of projects have a failure rate estimated as high as 60 percent. The two main causes for these high-cost failures are poor project management and poor change management. IBM, for example, launched eleven reengineering projects, the focus of which varied from the way it manages internal information systems to the way it developed products and served customers. "We have reduced IT spending by 31 percent for a total savings of more than $2 billion," the company reports. "Since 1993, cycle time for large systems development has been slashed from 56 months to 16 months. For low-end systems, it's seven months—down from two years."

Why Projects Fail

There are specific reasons why projects fail:

■ Failure to adhere to committed schedule due to:
   ☐ Variances
   ☐ Exceptions
   ☐ Poor planning
   ☐ Delays
   ☐ Scope creep

■ Poor resource utilization caused by:
   ☐ Lack of proper skills
   ☐ Poor time utilization
   ☐ Misalignment of skills and assignments

■ The projects portfolio was not managed correctly:
   ☐ The wrong projects were selected
   ☐ High-risk projects were not identified
   ☐ There was poor control over interdependencies between projects

■ Loss of intellectual and/or knowledge capital caused by:
   ☐ Lack of means to transfer knowledge
   ☐ People leaving the organization

■ People who use the output from the project are unprepared (i.e., change management)

The Professional Project Manager

We liken project management to quality management. Everyone thinks he or she knows what quality is, so organizations assume that anyone can manage quality. This same thought pattern applies to project management, but just as a quality manager is a special type of professional, so is a project manager. Project managers require skill, training, and effective leadership specifically related to project management.

The project management body of knowledge defines sixty-nine different tools that a project manager must master. Few project managers have mastered all of these tools. In today's complex world, most organizations have numerous projects going on at the same time. Many of them are interlinked and interdependent. Their requirements and schedules are continuously changing, which causes a chain reaction throughout the organization. For this reason, organizations can't afford to manage each project in isolation. They must instead manage their project portfolios, making the appropriate trade-offs of personnel and priorities.

Figure P.3 Integrated Management Tools

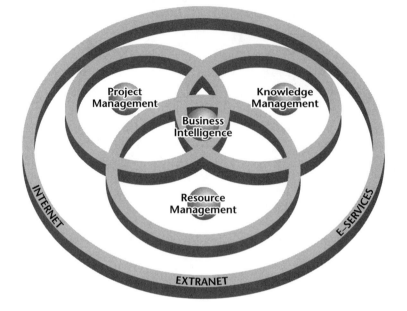

Project Management Excellence: The Art of Excelling in Project Management, book two in this series, focuses on how to use project management tools to effectively manage an organization's projects and integrate them into the total operations. This requires the effective integration of projects, resources, and knowledge to obtain business intelligence. (See figure P.3.)

PILLAR III—CHANGE MANAGEMENT EXCELLENCE

> "Research confirms that as much as 60 percent of change initiatives and other projects fail as a direct result of a fundamental inability to manage their social implications."
>
> —Gartner Group

We all like to think of ourselves as change masters, but, in truth, we are change bigots. Everyone in the management team supports change. They want to see others change, but when it comes to the managers themselves changing, they are reluctant to move away from past experiences that have proven successful for them. If an organization is going to change, top management must be the first to do so.

Change is inevitable, and we must embrace it if we are going to be successful in the challenging world in which we live. In *Change Management Excellence: The Art of Excelling in Change Management*, book three in this series, we discuss a change management system that is made up of three distinct elements:

■ Defining what will be changed
■ Defining how to change
■ Making the change happen

Most of the books written to date about change management have been theoretical in nature. They talk about black holes, cascading sponsorships, and burning platforms, but these are only the last phase of the change process. Most organizations don't understand or follow a comprehensive change management system. An effective change management system requires that the organization step back and define what will be changed. It's not about reducing stock levels, increasing customer satisfaction, or training people; it's about the fundamentals. Which of the key business drivers must be changed, and how do they need to be changed?

You must develop crisp vision statements that define how key business drivers will be changed over time. This requires that the organization have an excellent understanding of what its business drivers are and how they are currently operating. Then the organization must define exactly how it wants to change these key business drivers over a set period of time. Once the organization has defined what it wants to change, then it can define how to change. During this stage, the organization looks at the more than 1,100 different improvement tools that are available today, determines which tools will bring about the required changes to these key business drivers, and schedules the implementation of these tools and methodologies. This schedule makes up a key part of the organization's strategic business plan.

The last phase in the change management process is making the change happen. This is the area where behavioral scientists have developed a number of excellent approaches to break down resistance and build up resiliency throughout the organization. It is this phase that most change management books have concentrated on, but it is the last phase in the total change management system. Book three of this series focuses on all three phases, discussing in detail how to define what will be changed, defining how to change it, and how to make the change happen.

> "We [Japan] will win and you [USA] will lose. You cannot do anything about it because your failure is an internal disease. Your companies are based on Taylor's principles. Worse, your heads are Taylorized, too. We have passed the Taylor stage. We are aware that business has become terribly complex. Survival is very uncertain in an environment filled with risk, the unexpected, and competition."
> —**Konosuke Matsushita**
> **Founder,**
> **Matsushita Electric**
> **Industrial Co.**

PILLAR IV—KNOWLEDGE MANAGEMENT EXCELLENCE

"When a person dies, a library is lost."
—HJH

Today, more than ever before, knowledge is the key to organizational success. To fulfill this need, the Internet and other information technologies have provided all of us with more information than we can ever consume. Instead of having one or two sources of information, the Internet provides us with hundreds, if not thousands, of inputs, all of which must be researched for that key nugget of information. We are overwhelmed with so much information that we don't have time to absorb it.

To make matters worse, most of an organization's knowledge is still undocumented; it rests in the minds and experiences of its employees. This knowledge disappears from the organization's knowledge base whenever an individual leaves an assignment. In *Knowledge Management Excellence: The Art of Excelling in Knowledge Management*, book four in this series, we define how to establish a knowledge management system (KMS) that will be designed to sort out unneeded and/or false information and capture the "soft" knowledge needed to run an organization.

Because an almost endless amount of information clogs our computers, desks, and minds, a KMS must be designed around the organization's key capabilities and competencies.

What Is Knowledge?

Knowledge is a mixture of experiences, practices, traditions, values, contextual information, expert insight, and sound intuition that provides an environment and framework for evaluating and incorporating new experiences and information.

There are two types of knowledge: explicit and tacit.

Explicit knowledge is defined as knowledge that is stored in a semistructured medium, such as in documents, e-mail, voice mail, or video media. We like to call this hard or tangible knowledge. It is conveyed from one person to another in a systematic way.

Tacit knowledge is defined as knowledge that is formed around intangible factors embedded in an individual's experience. It is personal, content-specific knowledge that resides in an individual. It is knowledge that an individual gains from experience or skills that he or she develops. It often takes the form of beliefs, values, principles, and morals. It guides the individual's actions. We like to call this soft knowledge. It's embedded in the individual's ideas, insights, values, and judgment. It is only accessible through direct corroboration and communication with the individual who has the knowledge.

Knowledge management is defined as a proactive, systematic process by which value is generated from intellectual or knowledge-based assets and disseminated to the stakeholders. In *Knowledge Management Excellence* we will discuss the six phases required to implement an effective KMS. These are:

■ Phase 1—Requirements definition (seven activities)
■ Phase 2—Infrastructure evaluation (sixteen activities)
■ Phase 3—Knowledge management system design and development (twelve activities)
■ Phase 4—Pilot (fifteen activities)
■ Phase 5—Deployment (ten activities)
■ Phase 6—Continuous improvement (one activity)

"Knowledge takes us from chance to choice."
—HJH

The true measure of success for knowledge management is the number of people who access and implement ideas from the knowledge networks. These networks bring state-of-the-art ideas and/or best practices into the workplace. This allows the organization to develop areas of critical mass to implement standards that work. It also provides access for all employees—allowing them to make comments to improve those standards. Even the newest employee can look at the materials and make recommendations based upon personal insight, creativity, and experience.

A big challenge related to implementing a KMS is transforming knowledge held by individuals, including process and behavioral knowledge, into a consistent technological format that can be easily shared with the organization's stakeholders. However, the biggest challenge is changing the organization's culture from a knowledge-hoarding culture to a knowledge-sharing one.

PILLAR V—RESOURCE MANAGEMENT EXCELLENCE

"Even the best ideas need resources to transform them into profit."
—HJH

Nothing can be accomplished without resources. They lie at the heart of everything we do. If we have too few, we fail; if there are too many, there is waste—hindering the organization's competitive ability. Too many organizations limit their definition of resources to people and money. These are important, but they are only a small part of the resources an organization must manage. In *Resource Management Excellence: The Art of Excelling in Resource Management*, book five in this series, we look at all of the resources available to an organization and how to manage them effectively.

When resource management is discussed, it's in the broadest sense—all the resources and assets that are available to the organization. This includes stockholders, management, employees, money, suppliers, inventory, boards of directors, alliance partnerships, real estate, knowledge, customers, patents, investors, goodwill, and brick and mortar. When all of these are considered, it quickly becomes apparent that effective resource management is one of the most critical, complex activities within any organization. Managers and employees must examine their own performances to be sure they're doing the best they can.

Jack Welch, former CEO of General Electric, has created the following "Six Rules for Self-Examination":

1. Face reality as it is, not as it was or as you wish it were.
2. Be candid with everyone.
3. Don't manage; lead.
4. Change before you have to.
5. If you don't have a competitive advantage, don't compete.
6. Control your own destiny, or someone else will.

Each resource must be managed in its own special way to assist in building an excellent organization. The big question is, "How do you pull all these different activities and improvement approaches together and prioritize them?" To answer this, we will present a thorough, total-involvement approach to strategic planning, one that involves everyone—from the chairman of the board to the janitor, from sales to personnel, from development engineering to maintenance. Yes, this is a total-involvement approach to strategic planning; it is both bottom up and top down.

A total strategic planning process (i.e., business plan) has three main objectives. (See figure P.4.)

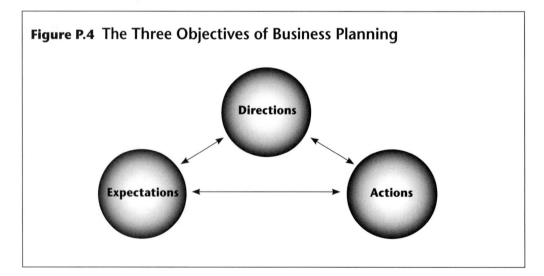

Figure P.4 The Three Objectives of Business Planning

Eleven documents are needed in a comprehensive, strategic business plan:

- Mission statement
- Value statements
- Organization's vision statements
- Strategic focus
- Critical success factors
- Objectives
- Goals
- Strategies
- Tactics
- Budgets
- Performance plans

"We expect a lot—highly motivated people consciously choosing to do whatever is in their power to ensure every customer is satisfied . . . and more. Every day. Without this concentrated effort, attempting a flawless service is really quite futile."
—Fred Smith
Founder and CEO,
Federal Express

Resource management can't be an afterthought; all executive decisions must be based upon it. It requires a lot of planning, coordination, reporting, and continuous refining to do an excellent job. Too many organizations manage operations by simply throwing more resources into the pot. They may be successful with this approach as long as they have little competition, but even the giants fail if they don't do an outstanding job of resource management.

THE SKY IS NOT THE LIMIT

"You are only limited by what you can envision."
—HJH

We used to say, "The sky's the limit" when we were thinking of the limits of possibility. Today there is no limit—if you can dream it or imagine it, then you can do it, or there is someone who can do it for you.

The world is different today than it was yesterday, and it will be even more different tomorrow. We live in a business environment that is advancing at an incredible pace. The things that were impossible yesterday are being done today and will be obsolete tomorrow. What was once purely science fiction is now possible, and even being accomplished. For example:

- *Colonization of Mars.* The most comprehensive plans to date have been created by the University of Houston's Sasakawa International Center for Space Architecture, under Larry Bell's direction. To create a foundation for sustainable Mars project growth, Bell's program has gone beyond developing a road map for creating the first colony; it has set up a formal training program for the first generation of space architects. Bell believes that colonizing Mars will be relatively easy. His major problem is convincing NASA that chemical propulsion is obsolete. "We need a launch vehicle about eight times bigger than the shuttle," he told *Popular Mechanics*. "I happen to believe the systems we are using are dinosaurs. We have to move beyond chemical propulsion."

- *Creating dinosaurs.* Until recently we believed that centuries of deterioration had so damaged critical genes in dinosaur DNA samples that it would be impossible to reconstruct the original animal. Recently, Belinda S.W. Chang, a professor at Rockefeller University in New York City, solved the missing DNA problem by building an artificial gene. It is believed to be identical to one that existed in the eye of an archosaurus, which lived 240 million years ago. The statistical analysis methods that she used in determining the DNA sequence of the rhodopsin gene opens a new frontier in reconstructing ancient genes.

- *Synthetic humans.* Within the next few years biomedical engineers will clear their final technological hurdle and hardwire sensors directly to nerves. A typical example of the work going on in this area is at Sandia National Laboratories in Albuquerque, New Mexico, where a chip has been developed that will synthesize the eye's retina. This holds the promise of restoring sight to thousands of people.

- *Altering gravity.* For years, antigravity and gravity shielding has been a favorite subject of science fiction writers, but professional physicists turned their backs on the concept, believing it impractical. A first step in tearing down these beliefs was accomplished by a former University of Alabama researcher, who successfully constructed a superconducting disc, which is essential in creating a gravity-altering force.

- *Teleportation. Star Trek's* Capt. James T. Kirk's famous line, "Beam me up, Scottie," might be a routine command in the future. Teleporting massless photons is now a reality. Transporting a single atom is the next step. In 2003 Ping Koy Lam at the Australian National University reached a major milestone in this objective. He successfully transported a beam of light.

As these examples demonstrate, we must start thinking differently. The word "impossible" should be stricken from our vocabulary. Thinking outside of the box is not good enough; we must tear down the walls of the box and build a culture without walls.

Our workforce is becoming more mobile. Organizations are cutting back by outsourcing all but their core capabilities and competencies. Business offices are shrinking as increasingly large numbers of people telecommute from their homes. No organization can afford to do that one-of-a-kind job with its own people, not when consultants can do it faster, better, and with reduced risk.

WHY DO YOU NEED ORGANIZATIONAL EXCELLENCE?

Times have changed, and our thinking about the way we manage our improvement activities must change with them. Only the very best organizations will attract customers in today's competitive environment. Producing excellent products isn't enough today; we must excel in all aspects of our organization. Piecemeal approaches such as TQM, Six Sigma, and customer relationship management must give way to a holistic view of the organization and its improvement efforts. An organization should wow its customers, not just satisfy them. Customers should rate the total organization as outstanding, not just very good.

Customers remember an organization's name for two reasons and for two reasons only:

- If it produces a poor product or service
- When it produces an exceptional product or service that makes them say, "Wow! That was a great experience."

> **"We must simply learn to love change as much as we have hated it in the past."**
> **—Tom Peters**
> ***Thriving on Chaos***

If you simply meet your customers' requirements, you do not build customer loyalty. They can be attracted away from you if your competition undercuts you by a few cents. Your organization must radiate excellence in everything it does.

For the last fifty years, the quality professional, management professional, and consultant have tried—largely unsuccessfully—to impose improvement systems on business, government, and academia. Consider the following attempts:

- Quality control—failed
- Total quality control—failed
- Zero defects—failed
- Total quality management—failed
- Process reengineering—failed
- Six Sigma—failing
- ISO 9001:2000—added little real value

The question is, "Why, after great spurts of success, do these sound improvement systems fall into oblivion?" They are much like an old toy that gets put back in the dark corner of the closet when a new toy is found under the Christmas tree.

These exercises in futility stem from applying improvement initiatives to an organization as if they were bandages. What's really needed is fundamental organizational change. Treating symptoms usually doesn't affect a cure; it just prolongs the agony.

These approaches failed because the initiatives were applied as separate activities instead of with the intention of making a total organizational transformation. It's similar to giving a person who has pneumonia an aspirin for his or her headache, thinking it will cure the disease.

From decade to decade, our business focus continually changes:

- 1970s—people
- 1980s—teams
- 1990s—processes
- 2000s—knowledge and adaptability

In keeping with these changes in focus, the approaches to performance improvement have also changed:

- ISO 9001 and ISO 14001—process-driven, lacking in business focus
- Total quality management (TQM)—process-driven, with statistical analysis and teams that are customer-focused
- National quality awards—quality-driven, plus results
- Six Sigma—problem/solution-driven, with a customer focus
- Total improvement management (TIM)—performance-driven/total organization-driven sales, marketing development, personnel, and production. It included organizational change.

  - Organizational excellence—performance-driven, including processes, projects, organizational change, information technology, resources, and knowledge management

"Only 5 percent of the organizations in the West truly excel. Their secret is not what they do, but how they do it."

—HJH

The following list gives a point score to these approaches' effectiveness in improving organizational performance.

- Casual—no recognized system . . . . 0 points
- ISO 9001 and ISO 14001—minimum requirements . . . . 200 points
- Six Sigma—problem-focused . . . . 400 points
- TQM—"womb to tomb" quality and teams . . . . 500 points
- National quality awards—results-based . . . . 600 points
- TIM—combined quality, reliability, performance, and results . . . . 800 points
- Organizational excellence—five pillars . . . . 1,000 points

"You can win the national quality award with 600 points out of a maximum of 1,000 points. That's 60 percent of the way to the goal."

—HJH

You might ask, "Where are we today?" A survey conducted by Harris Interactive Europe for Dow Corning provides us with the 2003 status. It included sixty-nine executives from a wide range of industries in the Americas, Europe, and Asia. This survey revealed that TQM was the most important business innovation for these organizations during the last three years. Although Six Sigma has received a lot of press during the past eight years, it did not rate in the top three most important business innovations. The top three, in descending order, are:

- TQM
- Process engineering
- Supply chain management

The American Society for Quality recently sponsored a survey of 600 executives from manufacturing, service, government, health care, and education. The survey reported that 99 percent of the executives surveyed believe that quality contributed to the bottom line. Also, it indicated that 92 percent of the executives believe that an organizationwide effort to use quality techniques provides a positive return. Figure P.5 gives a breakdown of the most frequently used quality techniques.

The survey indicates that a wide gap exists between the executives' awareness of quality improvement processes and their implementation. Again, the survey reveals that TQM is used 300 percent more than Six Sigma. The quality profession suffers by continuously changing the name of its activities despite little change in content.

"We want to operate far more efficiently. We want to operate at a new level of excellence."
—Robert J. Herbold
Former COO,
Microsoft

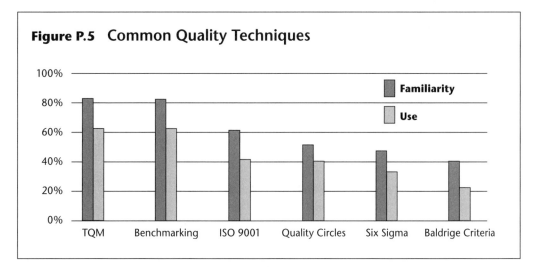

Figure P.5   Common Quality Techniques

ORGANIZATIONAL EXCELLENCE SUMMARY

"Being good is good. Being the best is great!"

—HJH

"The sizeable gap between usage and awareness leads me to believe that businesses and organizations either don't use quality methodologies to improve their operations, or they just don't realize that the processes they have in place are attributable directly to the quality discipline."

—Ken Case
Former president,
American Society for Quality

When we look at the five pillars that must be managed to achieve excellence, we see common threads that run through all of them:

- Communication
- Teamwork
- Empowerment
- Respect for one another
- Honesty
- Leadership
- Quality
- Fairness
- Technology

All of these key factors are built into the word "management." They turn an employee into an individual who owns his or her job, thereby bringing satisfaction and dignity to the individual for a job well done.

In today's worldwide marketplace, customers don't have to settle for second best. Overnight mail brings the best to everyone's doorstep. The Internet allows people to shop internationally, making it easy for them to get the best quality, reliability, and price, no matter who offers it. Customers are concerned about the products they purchase, but they

"The essence of competitiveness is liberated when we make people believe that what they think and do is important—and then get out of their way while they do it."

—Jack Welch
Former CEO,
General Electric

are equally or more concerned about dealing with organizations that care, are quick to respond, and that will listen and react to their unique needs. This means that to succeed in the 21st century organizations must excel in all parts of their businesses. Your organization must excel at what it does, but its stakeholders must also recognize your efforts as excellent. This will win over today's savvy customers.

CHAPTER 1

INTRODUCTION TO PROCESS MANAGEMENT EXCELLENCE

"To proceed without a process is to recede."
—HJH

Process management is not new to management or the quality professional. It is the basis of most quality improvement methodologies. The object of any process improvement activity is to understand, document, control, and reduce variation throughout the processes within the organization. Processes, by definition, are a "series of interconnected activities that takes an input, adds value to it, and produces an output." In essence, this is how all organizations function day-to-day. Your processes define how your organization operates. There are literally hundreds, if not thousands, of processes going on daily in all organizations. Figure 1.1 shows a simple process model.

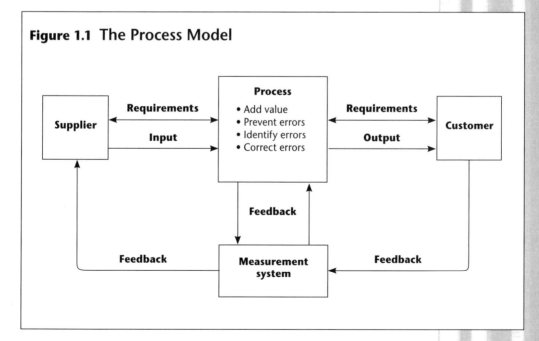

Figure 1.1 The Process Model

Using the model, we can see that to manage a process the following must be defined:

- An output requirement statement agreed upon by both the process owners and the customer
- An input requirement statement agreed upon by both the process owners and the suppliers
- An effective group of activities that transforms the supplier's input into an output that meets the customer's performance and quality requirements
- Feedback measurement systems between the customer and the process as well as the process and the suppliers
- The way people are trained to understand the process
- A measurement system within the process

These six key factors should be addressed when any process is designed. The problem facing most organizations is that many of their support processes were never designed in the first place. They were created out of need, without a real understanding of what a process is. Figure 1.2 provides a more detailed look at a typical process and its inputs and outputs.

"If you don't have your processes controlled, their output is a matter of luck."

—HJH

UNDERSTANDING THE PROCESS HIERARCHY

Almost everything we do or involve ourselves in is a process. There are highly complex processes that involve thousands of people (e.g., electing the president of the United States) and simple processes that require only seconds of your time (e.g., casting your ballot). Because of these differences, we must establish a process hierarchy. (See figure 1.3.)

From the macro view, processes are the key activities required to manage and/or run an organization. New product definition is a good example of a macro process.

A macro process can be divided into subprocesses that are logically related sequential activities that contribute to the mission of the macro process. Selecting a presidential candidate is a good example of a subprocess of the macro process of electing a president of the United States.

Often, complex macro processes are divided into a number of subprocesses to minimize the time required to improve the macro process and/or to provide particular focus on a problem, a high-cost area, a long-delay area, or to focus on continuous improvement.

Every macro process or subprocess is made up of a number of activities (e.g., assessing the status of a meeting room to determine whether it is ready for a focus group meeting). Activi-

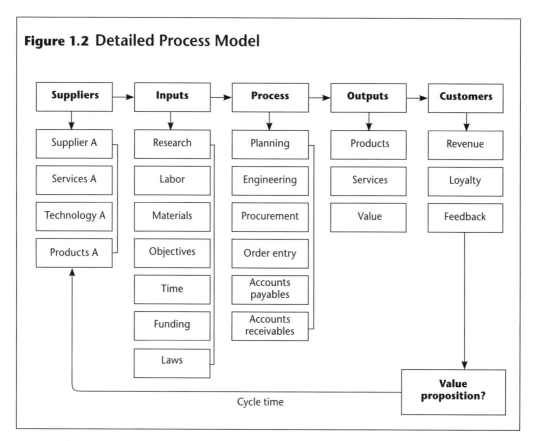

Figure 1.2 Detailed Process Model

ties are things that go on within all processes. As the name implies, they are the actions required to produce a particular result. Activities make up the major part of flowcharts.

Each activity is made up of a number of tasks. For example, some of the tasks that are part of checking out the focus group conference room would be ascertaining that:

- There are sufficient chairs for the invited guests.
- Water and ice are in each of the pitchers.
- A pen or pencil is placed on the table in front of each chair.

Normally, tasks are performed by an individual or small teams. They make up the very smallest, or micro, view of the process. Professor Robert Reid applied this process-hierarchy breakdown to getting up in the morning. (See figure 1.4.)

Key Process Definitions

- *Systems*—groups of related processes that may or may not be connected
- *Process*—a series of logically interconnected, related activities that takes an input, adds value to it, and produces an output for an internal or external customer

Figure 1.3 Process Hierarchy

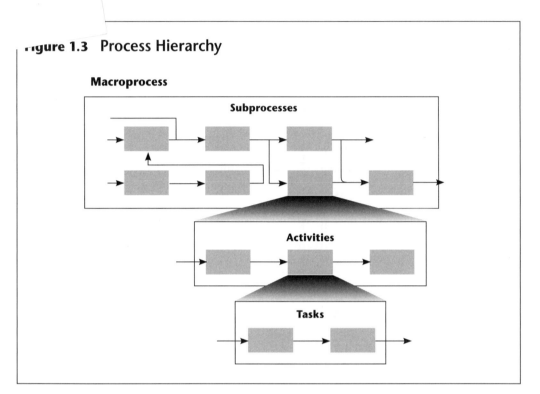

- *Activities*—small parts of a process usually performed by a single department or individual
- *Tasks*—steps that are required to perform a specific activity
- *External customer*—an individual or organization outside the supplier's organization that receives a product, a service, or information from the supplier
- *Internal customer*—a person, process, or department within the organization that receives output from another person and/or process within the same organization
- *Process effectiveness*—the extent to which the outputs of the process or subprocess meet the needs and expectations of its customers. This is much like quality, but more inclusive. Effectiveness is having the right output at the right place, at the right time, at the right price.
- *Process efficiency*—the extent to which resources are minimized and waste is eliminated in the pursuit of effectiveness. Productivity is a measure of efficiency.
- *Process adaptability*—the flexibility of the process to handle future, changing customer expectations and today's individual, special customer requests. This requires managing the process to meet today's special needs as well as future requirements. Adaptability is an area largely ignored, but it's critical for gaining a competitive edge in the marketplace. Customers always remember how you handled, or didn't handle, their special needs.

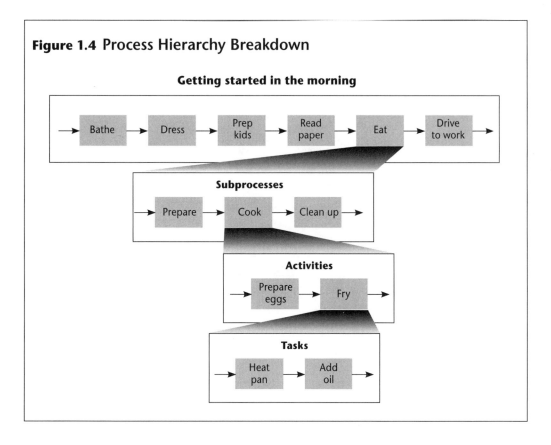

Figure 1.4 Process Hierarchy Breakdown

Identifying the Organization's Major Processes

It's important that an organization identifies, documents, and measures the adaptability, efficiency, and effectiveness of the major processes that drive it, provide output to the external customer, or consume large quantities of its resources. Figure 1.5 provides a picture of an enterprise process model.

Note that inputs can come from suppliers and investors or can be internally directed to the organization in the form of capital, human resources, technology, material, and information.

Due to changing regulations and global competition, continuous pressure is applied to systems and processes to improve. Improvement pressure also is applied by stakeholders who are looking to improve the benefits they receive from the organization. On the right-hand side of figure 1.5 are the internal and external customers whose needs are becoming more demanding.

Figure 1.6 divides the organization's systems into six process groupings that apply to many organizations. To define your major processes, look at each of these six groups and make a list of the major processes that are used in each group.

Figure 1.5 Process Definitions

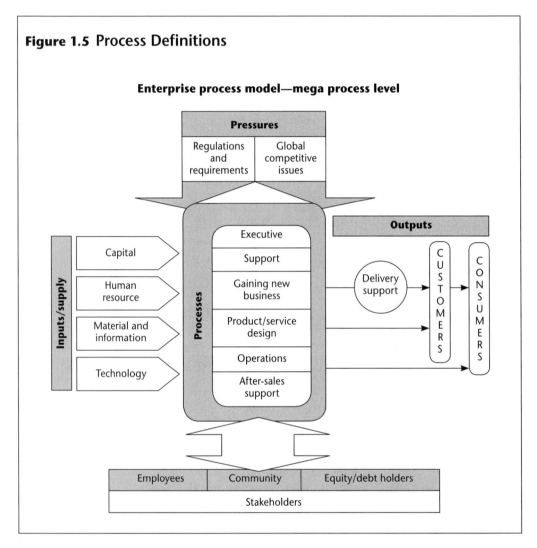

To establish a list of the organization's major processes, knowledgeable representatives from each of the organization's functions should meet to prepare a comprehensive list. For each of the systems and/or processes groupings, the organization should have a list of all of the major processes that are included in that group. It's best to limit the list for each group to fewer than twenty and more than three. All processes must have an input that triggers the start of the process's workflow and a definable output that goes to an internal or external customer.

The American Productivity and Quality Center defines thirteen major classifications of processes:

■ Understand markets and customers processes
■ Develop vision and strategy processes

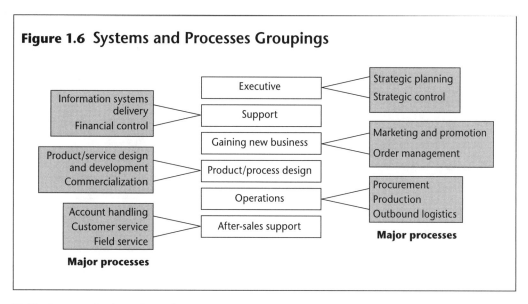

Figure 1.6 Systems and Processes Groupings

- Design products and services processes
- Marketing and sales processes
- Produce and deliver for manufacturing-oriented organizations processes
- Produce and deliver for service-oriented organizations processes
- Invoice and service customers processes
- Develop and manage human resources processes
- Manage information resources processes
- Manage financial and physical resources processes
- Execute environmental management program processes
- Manage external relationships processes
- Manage improvement and change processes

Sometimes an organization will begin with this list of major classifications and add their major processes related to each classification.

Xerox Corp. divides its processes into seventeen categories, as shown in figure 1.7.

A typical organization will list between forty to 120 major processes, or even up to 200. This number can be narrowed down to focus on the critical major processes within the organization. Typically, there are between twenty to forty critical major processes. Appendix B lists 140 typical business processes.

More than 80 percent of an organization's business processes are repetitive—things done over and over. These repetitive processes (white-, blue-, and gray-collar) can and should be controlled much the same way as manufacturing processes are controlled. We manage many business processes that are more complex than manufacturing processes.

Figure 1.7 Process Categories at Xerox Corp.

Categories	Number of Processes
1. Asset management	2
2. Billing and collection	5
3. Business management	12
4. Customer engagement	9
5. Financial management	9
6. Human resource management	9
7. Information management	4
8. Information technology management	6
9. Legal services	4
10. Logistics to inventory management	10
11. Market management	10
12. Order fulfillment	7
13. Product design and engineering	5
14. Product maintenance	9
15. Product operations	3
16. Supplier management	4
17. Technology management	5
Total	**113**

In the past, most of our attention was directed at process controls for the manufacturing area only. Today, the real payoff comes from applying proven manufacturing controls and feedback techniques to all activities in a business. We've learned to treat the entire organization as a complex operation containing many processes, only a small part of which are processes that produce the product sold to the customer. During the 1990s, a major change in organizational philosophy occurred, and management began to realize that it was responsible for leading a process revolution throughout the entire organization.

THE TWO APPROACHES TO PROCESS MANAGEMENT

There are two basic approaches to managing processes. They are:

- The micro-level approach, which is directed at managing processes within a natural work team or an individual department
- The macro-level approach, which is directed at managing processes that flow across departments and/or functions within the organization

Both of these approaches are good, and a combination of both should be used in most organizations.

The micro-level approach provides a personal understanding of the process; it focuses on the key measurements that employees are involved in, down to the task level. It's a comprehensive approach and builds process ownership throughout the organization. It's an excellent approach when you are focusing on continuous improvement within the process. The disadvantages of the micro-level approach are that it's directed at the sub-processes within an area and can lead to suboptimization for the overall process.

The macro-level approach looks at a process from the standpoint of the entire organization. This approach usually focuses only on the key business processes that flow across different functions within the organization. A typical organization will have between twenty to forty critical major processes. Managing these major processes is much more difficult than for subprocesses, not only due to their increased complexity, but also because, in most organizations, no one person is responsible for the overall performance of each major process.

BASIC ELEMENTS OF PROCESS MANAGEMENT

Both macro- and micro-level approaches have some characteristics in common. They all:

- Have customers who have defined output requirements
- Have documented processes
- Have suppliers who have defined input requirements
- Have documented measurements of efficiency
- Have a defined mission or purpose
- Have cost of errors measured
- Prevent errors. (This means that a process must be designed so that errors are difficult, if not impossible, to create.)
- Understand the capabilities of each activity within the process to produce acceptable output on schedule. (This can be accomplished through process capability studies.)

- Identify negative changes in the process so that they can be corrected before the process goes out of control. (Control charts do this well.)
- Ensure that controls are in place so that new employees are trained adequately before they start working in the process
- Are able to detect errors that result from activities within the processes that aren't capable of producing acceptable quality levels
- Report the errors that are detected
- Define the root cause of the errors and have a process to eliminate these root causes
- Obtain feedback information from customers that define the errors that the process lets slip through
- Develop ongoing feedback to their supplier about the outputs' acceptability and obtain the supplier's plan to eliminate unacceptable inputs to the process
- Reduce variation
- Measure improvement in reduced cost per item processed, reduced cycle time, and the level of customer satisfaction

As you can see, a process is almost like a small business when it comes down to managing it. All processes should be designed, documented, measured, and controlled. This is true of a chip manufacturing process as well as the hiring process or the accounts payable process. Most of the work that quality professionals have been involved in relates to controlling and continuously improving processes. Some of the tools they use are:

- Design of experiments
- Process capability studies
- Control charts
- Root cause analysis
- Document control
- Quality control circles
- Suggestion systems
- Six Sigma
- Shewhart's cycle
- ISO 9001
- Just-in-time
- *Kaizen*
- Supplier qualification

(See appendix A for definitions of these terms.)

CHAPTER II

THE TEAM APPROACH
TO CONTINUOUS IMPROVEMENT

"Although management reports 60 to 90 percent of their time is usually
spent in group activities, they also indicate that much of that time is
wasted or ineffectively used and that they get little or no training in skills
needed to work efficiently in groups."

—Kenneth Blanchard, Ph.D.
The One-Minute Manager series

Typically, process management should result in an overall improvement of between
5 to 15 percent per year in value added per employee, poor-quality cost, and quality.
This improvement should largely be driven by teams of employees and managers working together to solve problems and taking advantage of improvement opportunities. If a
5- percent improvement looks small, just look at what a 5-percent reduction in cost would
have done for each of the organizations shown in figure 2.1.

**Figure 2.1 Percent Increase in Profits if the Organization Reduced
Cost by 5 Percent**

In millions of U.S. dollars

Organization	Revenues	Profits	5-percent improvement savings	Potential profit	Percent improvement in profit
Wal-Mart Stores	$219,812	$6,671	$10,990	$17,661	165%
General Motors	$177,260	$601	$8,863	$9,464	1475%
Ford	$162,412	-$5,453	$8,121	$2,668	∞
Verizon	$67,190	$389	$3,360	$3,749	864%
Hewlett-Packard	$45,266	$408	$2,263	$2,671	555%
Kmart	$36,910	-$95	$1,846	$1,751	∞

For the past thirty years the involvement of employees in designing their work processes and in solving problems related to these processes has fostered the increased use of teams. This movement has benefited organizations by:

- Building cooperation
- Building understanding
- Aligning employees' and the organization's goals
- Reducing cycle time
- Reducing cost
- Improving quality
- Improving customer satisfaction
- Improving morale

The team movement's effect on organizations has varied from a negative impact to one of the key business success drivers. The difference between highly successful organizations and failures is not the basic concept but the way they implement the team process.

For a team to reach its full potential and maximize its efficiency and effectiveness, it must have the four Ts:

- Training
- Tools
- Time
- Team support

Teams take many forms, and each team structure operates using different guidelines and tools. For example, quality control circles need training on the seven basic problem-solving tools, while more advanced cross-functional business process improvement teams must have a thorough understanding of the seven basic problem-solving tools, plus the ten fundamental business process improvement tools.

TYPES OF TEAMS

The seven types of teams most often used in businesses today are:

- Department improvement team (DIT) or natural work team (NWT)
- Process improvement team (PIT)
- Task team (TT)
- Task force (TF)
- Quality control circle (QCC)
- Autonomous work team (AWT)
- Six Sigma team (SST)

All of these teams are used to continuously improve processes, with the exception of process improvement teams and some Six Sigma teams. Business process improvement teams and some Six Sigma teams work on projects that are designed to bring about drastic changes to processes in a very short period of time.

The chart shown in figure 2.2 points out the differences between the various types of teams.

> **"That [today's environment] requires a dramatic increase in the willingness of people to assemble themselves into cross-disciplinary teams that meet a need in the marketplace and then disband when that need has been satisfied."**
> **—Sam Palmisano**
> **CEO, IBM**

Department Improvement Team or Natural Work Team

One of the most valuable teams in the entire process, the DIT or NWT, is made up of the employees in a particular department reporting to the same manager.

Typically, these teams start by performing an area activity analysis to develop a mission, their customer set, and their measurements. If they have problems meeting their measurements, they are trained to solve them.

This type of team focuses on problems it has knowledge about and the resources to solve. It is empowered to implement the solutions with little or no outside approvals. This team is usually led by the department manager or supervisor. In cases where the department has more than ten employees, membership in the team may rotate every ninety to 180 days. This gives everyone a chance to participate.

The team meets for about one hour, once a week, for an indefinite period. Departmental problems are identified and prioritized. Management has the final veto in case the team selects a problem that is outside its scope or doesn't meet the return on investment requirements.

Because this team deals with issues that affect its own efficiency and effectiveness, huge opportunities exist for saving organizational resources.

Process Improvement Teams

> **"More than $800 million in savings last year [2003] came from employee-initiated process improvement teams."**
> **—Michael S. Dell**
> **Chairman and CEO,**
> **Dell Computer**

The PIT is another valuable team. Although other teams tend to have more of a task-oriented mission, PITs focus on specific processes. These are also called cross-functional teams.

Management or individuals intimately involved in a particular process select PIT members. In some cases, short meetings are held over long periods of time (typically one to two hours per week for three months or more). These PITs often identify process issues that can be corrected by a task team. Although the PIT remains together, the task team meets only until the particular process issue is resolved.

Often organizations will prioritize their critical business processes and assign PITs to redesign or reengineer one to three processes at a time. In these cases, the PIT members

Figure 2.2 Types of Teams and Their Characteristics

Characteristics	Department improvement team	Process improvement team	Task team	Task force	Quality control circle	Autonomous work team	Six Sigma team
Membership	Department members	Members involved in the process	Selected members based on experience	Selected members based on experience	Department members	Department members	Selected members based on experience
Participation	Mandatory	Mandatory	Mandatory	Mandatory	Voluntary	Voluntary	Mandatory
Management direction	Moderate	Moderate	Moderate	High	Low	Low	Low
Task selection	By team	By management	By management	By management	By team	By team	By Black Belt
Urgency	Moderate	Moderate	Moderate	High	Low	Moderate	Moderate
Scope of activity	Departmentwide	Processwide	Organizationwide	Organizationwide	Departmentwide	Departmentwide	Organizationwide
Activity time	Short meetings, intermediate period	Short meetings, intermediate period	Short meetings, long period	Long meetings, short period, no other assignment	Short meetings, ongoing	Short meetings, ongoing	Short meetings, long period
Process facilitator	Recommended	Recommended	Optional	Optional	Recommended	Recommended	None
Team leadership	Supervisor	Process owner or designee	Appointed	Appointed	Supervisor of designee	Shared or rotated	Black Belt
Implementation	By team	By team or others	By team or others	By others	By team	By team	By team or others

are usually assigned to the PIT for between 50 to 100 percent of their time for three to six months. Like the DIT, the PIT has great opportunities to reduce internal costs by increasing the efficiency, effectiveness, and adaptability of the process.

Task Teams

A TT is put together to resolve an issue and then disbanded. Management selects team members based on their experience with the issue. The issue and/or problem usually isn't urgent. The team assignment might consist of short meetings over long periods (e.g., one hour per week for thirty days or more) or, if the issue is of a more immediate nature, longer meetings over a short period.

Task Force

The TF is most often designed to work on an important issue or problem. It meets for long periods, sometimes for as long as twelve hours a day, seven days a week, for a short duration (typically thirty days or fewer). This team is usually called on to solve "survival" issues or problems that must be corrected or resolved as soon as possible. Usually, this team's activity takes precedence over all other activities in the organization. Typically, TF teams are formed when a manufacturing process is closed down for what could be a long time due to problems or a customer safety issue. The teams often are used to take advantage of a particular opportunity that will exist only for a short time. (For example, a customer wants to select a supplier of a costly item.)

Management usually forms the TF, and participation is mandatory. The leader and members are selected based on their experience with the issue at hand. Direction from management is as intensive as the deadline for resolving the issue is eminent.

The use of TFs indicates that management has major problems with the organization's processes. Organizations that have good business processes don't need to use TFs to manage and correct their problems because they will be eliminated or recognized before they become critical.

Quality Control Circles

The terms "quality control circles" and "quality circles" are used interchangeably and refer to the same organizational structure and activities. This is the team concept that allowed Japan to excel during the 1970s and 1980s. It also started the participative management movement in North America as we know it today. Unfortunately, QCCs got a bad reputation during the late 1970s and early 1980s because most North American organizations used the concept incorrectly. Management did not provide the required skills training, direction, and support for successful implementation. In addition, management expected the QCCs to solve problems that it had been unable to solve for years. As a result, management became discouraged with QCCs because they did not rack up big dollar savings. Yoshio Kondo, Ph.D., one of Japan's leading quality professors and consultants, stated, "Quality control circles are to motivate employees, not to reduce cost." Japan has been very effective in using QCCs to train its employees in how to solve problems. In North America, the QCC movement failed not because of the employees but because of management's lack of understanding of the process and, as a result, its misuse of it. As North American management matures, it will understand why QCCs are important to its overall success. (The self-managed work team concept is based upon the QCC concept.)

The QCC is made up of volunteers who hold short meetings during a definite period of time and work on either departmental or organizational issues. Management direction tends to be low with QCCs. This is probably what got North American QCC teams in trouble in the first place. The more management interest in the process, the more likely the team is to succeed. Most U.S. organizations have moved away from referring to a team as a QCC and, even if it is the exact same thing, call it something else. If and when U.S. organizations start to empower their employees, these are the types of teams that will most often be used. QCCs are a good lead into self-managed work teams and/or autonomous work teams.

Autonomous Work Teams

The AWT seems to be the "brass ring" many organizations are grabbing for. There is a future for AWTs in the United States, but it is limited.

This type of team often has been called a self-managed work team or a self-directed work team. In the truest sense, the AWT manages its own business without outside interference from upper management. The team is responsible for setting its own departmental budget, managing its own resources, and even hiring and firing its employees. Most organizations in the United States that use this type of team allow it to function with minimal direction from management. In some cases they function very effectively. Today, fewer organizations are using AWTs in the United States.

A word of caution: Although AWTs can be real moneymakers for certain organizations, they don't work for everyone. Before an organization implements this type of structure, it should be very far along with its quality improvement initiative, and there must be a high degree of trust between management and employees. This type of organizational structure is not for neophytes.

Six Sigma Teams

SSTs are formed to address a specific problem or opportunity. These usually are identified by a skilled, trained problem solver called a Black Belt. The Black Belt presents the problem to management and gets approval to form a SST. The Black Belt leads the SST; the other team members are called Green Belts.

Kevin B. Rollins, president of Dell Computer, personally oversees the Six Sigma process that is penetrating the organization, from marketing to manufacturing. It was estimated that Dell saved $1.5 billion in expenses during 2004, and Six Sigma played a big part in realizing these savings. Dell isn't concentrating its efforts on breakthrough savings. Its emphasis is on small savings in the areas of errors and waste. A typical example of the value of this "small savings" emphasis was the replacement of colored paper with plain white paper for parts lists, saving Dell $23,000 per year.

"Populist leaders encourage people to develop their own form of teamwork and their personal ownership of competitive improvements."
—Dr. Armand V. Feigenbaum CEO, General Systems Co.

MAKING TEAMS HUM

Of course, there are both bad and outstanding (i.e., ineffective and effective) teams of all kinds. It's not the type of team that determines if it's good or bad but other factors. These include:

- How well the team is managed
- How interested the team is in the subject
- How well the team is trained

Everyone on the team must have the right attitude for the team to excel.

In his *The One-Minute Manager* series, Kenneth Blanchard wrote that, for a team to excel, it must have seven characteristics, depicted by the acronym PERFORM:

- Purpose
- Empowerment
- Relationships and communication
- Flexibility
- Optimal productivity
- Recognition and appreciation
- Morale

"Of the seven characteristics, two are most important: optimal productivity and morale. To be a successful team, the group must have a strong ability to produce results and a high degree of satisfaction in working with one another."
—Kenneth Blanchard, Ph.D.
***The One-Minute Manager* series**

TRAINING TEAMS

In every organization, the topic that always makes the employees' top five list is training or the lack thereof. Most often it is their No. 1 issue. At Xerox, effective quality

"Every organization is a university. Even though executives, managers, and employees may be unaware of the fact (and most are), the organization's agenda creates a 'curriculum' that instructs and develops people to produce highly predictable results over time."
—William J. Schwarz CEO, CEO Alliance and the Center for Inspired Performance

improvement team participation grows, in part, from effective quality training. At a minimum, every Xerox employee has received twenty-eight hours of quality training. Xerox's initial training investment is estimated at more than four million employee hours and $125 million. Training teams is just as important as training individuals to do their jobs. There are really only two ways to train teams. Let's look at both.

Formal Classroom Training

Teams can be trained as a group or as individual participants, where several (normally ten to twenty) employees are trained together and assigned a team at a later date. Either way works well; however, in both cases the training should not be conducted until the participants are within thirty days of using what they have learned. Don't waste valuable organizational resources by training and waiting three to six months to put the training to use.

An additional word of caution: Timid or less aggressive team members might never become completely competent through this approach. Team and problem-solving training should be a part of the new-employee orientation process, providing everyone in the organization with a common language and approach.

For more than forty years, teams have been effectively used to solve problems. The approach varies, depending upon the problem and skills of the team. Teams should evolve through the following levels:

1. Seven basic problem-solving tools
2. Plan-do-check-act—the basic problem-solving cycle defined by Walter Shewhart
3. Same as No. 1 and No. 2 plus the seven management tools
4. Add statistical analysis and design of experiments
5. Add simulation modeling, structured analysis, and causal modeling
6. TRIZ (Russian acronym for "Theory of Inventive Problem Solving")

Of course, not all teams need to or should progress through all six problem-solving levels. In fact, most teams can stop at level two.

All employees should be trained in the seven basic problem-solving tools:

- Brainstorming
- Check sheets
- Graphs
- Nominal group technique
- Force field analysis
- Cause-and-effect diagrams
- Pareto diagrams

There are a number of other basic tools that every member of a formal team should be trained to use. These are:

- The five Ws and two Hs
- Delphi narrowing technique
- Failure mode and effects analysis
- The five Ss
- Histograms
- Milestone graphs
- Mind mapping
- The Shewhart cycle
- Root cause analysis
- Run charts

The more advanced teams must be trained in the seven new management tools. These are:

- Affinity diagrams
- Interrelationship diagrams
- Tree diagrams
- Matrix diagrams
- The prioritization matrix
- Process decision program charts
- Arrow diagrams

Process improvement teams, which are involved in reengineering, redesign, or benchmarking, should be trained in the following twelve basic business process improvement tools:

- Business process improvement concepts
- Flowcharts
- Interviewing techniques
- Value-added analysis
- Bureaucracy elimination method
- Process and paperwork simplification techniques
- Simple language analysis and improvement methods
- Process walkthrough methods
- Cost and cycle-time analysis
- Statistical process control
- Organizational change management
- Knowledge management

In addition, the process owners, who chair PITs, need to be trained in the twelve sophisticated tools. These are:

- Quality function deployment
- Program evaluation and review technique charting
- Business systems planning
- Process analysis technique
- Structured analysis and design
- Value analysis and control
- Information engineering
- Process benchmarking
- Poor quality cost
- Design of experiments
- Simulation modeling
- Project management

At the other end of the spectrum, Six Sigma teams use sophisticated problem-solving tools, including structured analysis and diagnostic tools. In most organizations all employees should be trained in the seven basic problem-solving tools even if they aren't assigned to a team.

On-the-Job Training

Actually, this should be called on-the-team training, as the more skilled or experienced team members train new members. Although this type of training is not as effective as formal classroom training, the new team member usually can catch up with the others. Here the untrained team member is taught the skills he or she needs by other, more skilled or experienced team members. Some organizations formalize their on-the-job training process by assigning a training curriculum for teams to follow. This ensures each new team member receives the same amount of training as the others. Obviously, the downside to this approach is having one or more team members who might not be as effective as other members with more formal training, which will slow down the rest of the team.

> **"Character and skill development is a process of ongoing improvement or progression, a constant upward spiral."**
> —**Stephen R. Covey, Ph.D.**
> *The Seven Habits of Highly Effective People*

UTILIZING OUTSIDE RESOURCES

Note: This subject matter was prepared by Brett Trusko, senior manager, Harrington Institute Inc.

The very nature of a process change implies that the organization recognizes a need or opportunity to do things differently and/or better than it does currently. One of the more difficult aspects of this realization is that the organization might need to employ the help of outside experts, who can be extremely expensive, and who don't possess the commitment to the organization that an insider might have.

Accordingly, though seldom used enough, insiders and virtual insiders can help to bridge the difference between what the organization can afford and what the consultant costs. This team of insiders and virtual insiders might include the following:

- Insiders who are part of the team
  - ☐ Distributed teams
  - ☐ Prophets and visionaries

"If people don't grow, the company doesn't grow."
—Steven Reinemund
CEO, PepsiCo. Inc.

- Insiders who aren't part of the team
  - ☐ Distributed employees of the organization
  - ☐ Employees of partner organizations
  - ☐ Subject-matter experts from other parts of the organization (i.e., management of intellectual capital)

- Outsiders who are part of the team
  - ☐ Free agents
  - ☐ Subject-matter experts
  - ☐ Boards of directors
  - ☐ Stringers (i.e., advocates who work with the organization at no cost)

- Outsiders who aren't part of the team
  - ☐ Thought leaders
  - ☐ Authors
  - ☐ Friends of the firm

Although the more traditional manager views the use of resources from outside the organization as inefficient, or worse, potentially damaging, the contemporary manager might see the use of nontraditional resources as efficient and an opportunity to import new ideas and talent without having to use high-priced consulting firms or limited research resources.

Insiders Who Are Part of the Team

These team members are often a forgotten part of the organization's resources because they are often remotely located and thus might be difficult to collaborate or "connect" with. These might be individuals who are a part of a remote or distributed team and who might be considered too extreme in their thinking or philosophy.

Distributed teams. These could include individuals and teams not located together. It's difficult enough to work with distributed teams, but it becomes more so when the project involves brainstorming, flowcharting, and a general collaborative effort. It's important to remember, however, that the distributed worker is an important team member and can offer insights into the working of the organization outside the traditional office. For example, it would be foolish for an organization to develop a sales cycle process without involving the remote salespeople who understand how the market really works. It's amazing how many organizations believe that processes which work in the United States will work in other parts of the world and wonder why they have process issues in those markets.

Prophets and visionaries. Most organizations have internal prophets and visionaries. Some companies prefer not to deal with these individuals, assuming they just don't understand day-to-day business. Others have no clue that such resources exist internally. Regardless, identifying these prophets and visionaries can accomplish two goals for the organization. First, these individuals are probably highly respected and can be a tremendous asset in fostering acceptance and adoption of change by the group. Second, these individuals, who might not be interested in the finer points of day-to-day operations, place process improvement in the context of the bigger picture. For example, it doesn't make much sense to design a process to best-of-breed today when the entire industry might be different in six months. Prophets and visionaries can help the team understand the challenges that must be addressed for the organization to succeed. They are required members of all reengineering projects.

Insiders Who Aren't Part of the Team

Several types of insiders are available who are part of the team but seldom used in an improvement effort. These employees might not be directly involved in strategy and implementation, but they will be required to work with the modified processes in the future. Their ability to work with the processes can mean the difference between success and failure. These are the employees who create the "hidden office" referred to in my book *Business Process Improvement* (McGraw-Hill, 1991).

Distributed employees of the organization. Although these employees might not be actively involved in your team, they are often the glue that holds a process together after a change. Involving these employees creates a sense of ownership of the process that can help to deter workarounds in the future. For example, if distributed insiders aren't included in discussions that change the way they work, why should they believe that anyone is interested in their opinions when they see problems with the redesigned processes?

Employees of partner organizations. Management literature often refers to partner organizations as "stakeholders" and as important to your business. Failing to include them in discussions about processes can mean disgruntled trading partners and a potential loss of future business. For example, consider the supplier that created specialized processes to address your organization's idiosyncrasies. It's likely that it spent considerable time and effort modifying its systems to deal with the way your organization does business. For you to change suddenly might cause its business to falter.

Alternatively, you could consider the trading partner as an entity with the opportunity to see how your competition's processes work. In interviewing those trading partners, you might find that your competitor has a process superior to yours (in working with trading partners), and that you can re-create and improve upon those processes in your own organization. Obviously, this approach can eliminate hours of work just getting to a baseline.

Subject-matter experts from other parts of the organization. In most organizations management of intellectual capital is almost nonexistent. For example, consider an organization that was having serious issues with employee loyalty and retention. The organization was quick to form a committee to find solutions to the problem but ignored the fact that it had an internal team that consulted with other organizations on the same subject. From a process improvement perspective, this resembles an organization that designs office environments but then hires a consultant to design its own office environment.

> "Many organizations find it beneficial to use outside consulting resources to freshen in-house ideas."
>
> —HJH

Outsiders Who Are Part of the Team

Organizations employ consultants to do many things, including:

- Training employees
- Installing information technology systems
- Benchmarking
- Process redesign or reengineering
- Building information systems to support new processes
- Mapping current processes
- Organizational change management
- Strategic planning
- Introducing new concepts
- Facilitating teams or meetings
- Helping with peak workloads

Outsiders increasingly make up a greater share of internal teams. Unfortunately, we often use them for tasks below their skill levels. Many consultants with advanced degrees and prestigious backgrounds work part of their time in high-powered positions and part of their time as lower-level managers. How many of these "experts" do you have in your organization? If you don't know, you aren't utilizing your company's full potential.

Free agents. Many highly trained individuals have chosen to be free agents. Although the free agency model offers them the ability to diversify their careers (thus insulating them from layoffs), many are frustrated because their skills are underutilized, and they aren't consulted in areas where they are considered experts in the industry. For example, a retired CFO for a Fortune 100 company was working part time as an advisor to a startup technology organization. When management decided to go public, it didn't ask this expert's opinion because it forgot what he did in his previous life. (A one-person consulting firm would be a free agent.)

Subject-matter experts. In this ever-more-complicated world, SMEs have become more common in organizations. Some are employed full time, and some act in the capacity of free agents. Although they might not be ideal candidates for a full-blown process improvement project because of their lack of training, they can be a valuable asset to the project as a consultant or advisor on specialized aspects of a process.

Boards of directors. It's likely that the makeup of the board of directors at most organizations will change because of the scandals that have rocked the markets in recent years. This will require board members to be more actively involved in the day-to-day activities of their organizations. If you already have an involved board, contact it for input regarding major processes and approaches to business problems. This involvement will draw upon the board's extensive experience with both the organization and the outside world.

Stringers. Stringers are paid on a retainer or on commission to be available to the organization when their skills are needed. For example, one individual carries five business cards and is listed as a principal employee on the Web sites of all five organizations. Although he is an important part of each organization, they all tend to see his responsibilities as outward-facing. The reality is that even in the case of commissioned employees, better internal processes mean more success for them in the long run, and they are happy to contribute to the organization's improvement efforts.

Outsiders Who Aren't Part of the Team

Outsiders are individuals who aren't part of the team but are interested in the team's assignments. It's amazing to see the number of individuals who pay to attend lectures by industry thought leaders and walk away with the attitude that the lecture was interesting but didn't apply to their business. Then they turn around two weeks later and hire a consultant because that person has a "developed methodology" for doing exactly what he or she heard the thought leader elaborate on in the first place.

Thought leaders. This is the organization's unpaid strategic planning department. Nine times out of ten a good thought leader knows more about the industry and its trends than the internal teams. By paying attention to these thought leaders, and planning direction based on well-thought-out leadership, an organization can save time and money by defining the future state in a change-management exercise prior to developing new processes.

Authors. These individuals, like thought leaders, are paid to take the pulse of the industry and report it to business professionals. Most authors are more than willing to discuss business and process problems with management and PITs. Many process teams do expensive research themselves because they mistakenly believe that outside experts are too expensive.

Friends of the firm. It's likely that your organization has more friends than it realizes. Friends of the firm might include consultants who want to build a portfolio and are willing to consult for a minimum fee, past employees who are still friendly, and past customers who have developed relationships with individuals inside your organization and would like to see them succeed.

Outside Resources Summary

Utilizing resources that aren't a part of the traditional PIT dramatically improves the chances of success. These resources include insiders who are part of the team, insiders who aren't part of the team, outsiders who are part of the team, and outsiders who aren't part of the team.

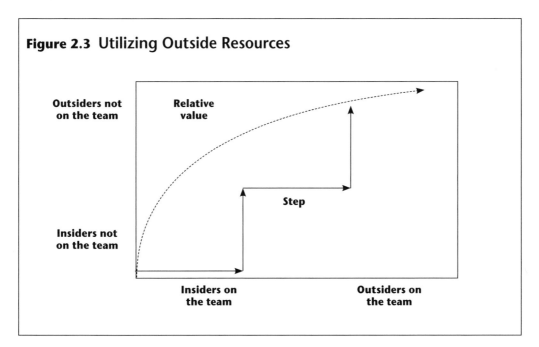

Figure 2.3 Utilizing Outside Resources

"To be a successful team, the group must have a strong ability to produce results and a high degree of satisfaction in working with one another."
—Kenneth Blanchard, Ph.D.
The One-Minute Manager **series**

The project manager must have excellent people and project management skills to manage a project involving people outside of his or her direct sphere of influence, but these skills can be learned by taking courses in managing distributed teams. The natural development progression that the project manager goes through is shown in figure 2.3.

First, a manager should take steps to engage insiders who would traditionally be on the team. Then the manager should try to involve insiders who aren't normally on the team. The next step is to involve outsiders by inviting them to become members of the team. Finally, outsiders who traditionally wouldn't be part of the team are involved. The total value to the organization is shown as a dotted line in figure 2.3.

The results that can be achieved by successfully identifying and mobilizing individuals outside the project can significantly reduce the cost of a process improvement project while increasing the quality of the results. Actual amounts saved will vary, based on the degree to which outsiders are used, in what capacity, and the nature and skills of such individuals. It's conceivable that savings achieved by engaging outsiders and distributed team members can approach 30 percent of the total project. By utilizing outside or nontraditional resources, the PIT will enhance its ability to convince senior management of the value of process improvement.

CHAPTER III

THE MICRO-LEVEL APPROACH TO PROCESS MANAGEMENT

"You need to know what your internal and external customers want and then give it to them."

—HJH

The micro-level approach to process management is the one most universally used. It is based upon the belief that the employee doing the job has the best understanding of it and therefore is in the best position to improve the process. The micro-level approach focuses on how members of a natural work team (NWT) or single department interact with each other, their customers, and their suppliers to conduct the duties assigned to the group. This approach brings people together into a tightly knit team. It has the advantage of acquainting everyone with the work that the group is performing and the problems the group is facing. There are two ways to implement micro-level improvements:

- Random micro-level approach
- Systematic micro-level approach

RANDOM MICRO-LEVEL APPROACH

Often, organizations train people to use problem-solving approaches such as:

- Brainstorming
- Check sheets
- Error-proofing
- Flowcharts
- Function diagrams
- Histograms
- Statistical process control
- Interrelationship diagrams
- Cause-and-effect diagrams

- Mind maps
- Pareto diagrams
- Run charts
- Scatter diagrams

However, when the training is finished, these individuals are simply turned loose to find problems to solve. This has led to extensive effort being expended on items that have little or no effect on organizational performance.

SYSTEMATIC MICRO-LEVEL APPROACH

The systematic micro-level approach establishes a set of measurements and performance standards that allows the NWT to focus its continuous improvement efforts on real problems that have a positive effect on the organization's overall performance. To best accomplish this, a methodology called area activity analysis is used.

AREA ACTIVITY ANALYSIS

Area activity analysis (AAA) is the best methodology for managing problems at the micro-level. The AAA methodology is used by NWTs to define key processes, including:

- The NWT's mission
- The NWT's major processes
- The customers for each major process and an agreed-upon output specification
- The suppliers for each major process and agreed-upon input specifications
- The internal process that converts the inputs into outputs
- The efficiency measurements for the process
- The measurement system

> "Imagine a team implementing a new idea each week and maintaining that idea through measurement systems and process controls."
> —**William J. Schwarz
> CEO, CEO Alliance and the Center for Inspired Performance**

Dividing this effort among the NWTs reduces the effort required by any one group and puts the process in the hands of the people who work with it.

The AAA methodology has been divided into seven different phases to make it simple for the NWT to implement. (See figure 3.1.) Each of these phases consists of steps that will progressively lead the NWT through the methodology.

Implementing the seven phases will bring about a major improvement in the organization's measurement systems, increase understanding and cooperation, and lead to reduced cost, reduced cycle time, and improved quality.

Phase 1—Preparation for AAA

AAA is most effective when it precedes other initiatives such as continuous improvement, team problem solving, total quality management, reengineering, or new information technology systems. It's also best to implement the AAA methodology throughout the organization. This doesn't mean that it won't work if other improvement activities are underway or if it's used only by one area. During the preparation phase, the pros and cons of implementing AAA within an organization should be evaluated. A decision can then be made whether to use AAA within the organization.

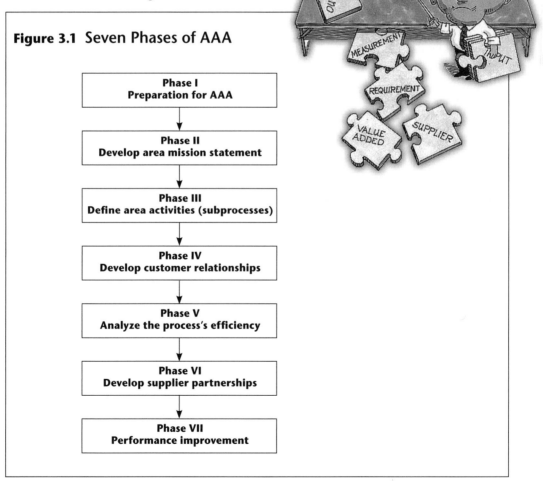

Figure 3.1 Seven Phases of AAA

Phase I
Preparation for AAA

↓

Phase II
Develop area mission statement

↓

Phase III
Define area activities (subprocesses)

↓

Phase IV
Develop customer relationships

↓

Phase V
Analyze the process's efficiency

↓

Phase VI
Develop supplier partnerships

↓

Phase VII
Performance improvement

Phase 1 is divided into five steps:

1. Analyze the environment.
2. Form an AAA project team.
3. Define the implementation process.
4. Involve upper management.
5. Communicate AAA objectives.

Phase 2—Develop Area Mission Statement

A mission statement documents the reasons for the NWT's or area's existence. It should be prepared before the NWT or area is formed, and it's usually changed only when the NWT or area decides to pursue a different set of activities. For the AAA methodology, a mission statement is a short paragraph, no more than two or three sentences, that defines the NWT's role and its relationships with the rest of the organization and/or the external customer.

Every NWT should have a mission statement that provides the NWT's manager and employees with guidance related to the activities on which the NWT should expend its resources. Standard good business practice calls for the NWT's mission statement to be prepared before the team is formed. The mission statement should be reviewed each time there is a change to the NWT's structure or responsibilities. It should also be reviewed about every four years, even if the NWT's structure has remained unchanged, to confirm that the mission statement reflects the current activities that are performed by the NWT.

During phase 2, the NWT's service policy is also developed. A service policy is a short statement that defines how the NWT will interface with its customers and suppliers.

During phase 2, the AAA team reviews and updates the NWT's mission statement, or writes one, if necessary. In all cases, any change to the mission statement must be approved by upper management before it's finalized.

Phase 2 is divided into six steps:

1. Obtain present mission statement.
2. Develop preliminary area mission statement (done by NWT's manager).
3. Develop preliminary area mission statement (done by each employee).
4. Develop a consensus draft area mission statement.
5. Finalize area mission statement.
6. Develop the area's service policy.

Phase 3—Define Area Activities (Subprocesses)

During this phase, the NWT will define the processes performed within the area. For each major process, the NWT will define each process's output(s) and the customers that receive that output. A process champion is assigned to each process.

Phase 3 is divided into eight steps:

1. Identify processes. (Each team member does this.)
2. Combine processes into broad process categories.
3. Develop percentage of time expended on processes.
4. Identify major processes.
5. Compare process list with area mission statement.
6. Align processes with mission.
7. Approve the area's mission statement and major processes.
8. Assign process champions.

Phase 4—Develop Customer Relationships

During this phase, the NWT meets with customers that receive the outputs from the major process conducted by the area. The purposes of this are to:

- Define the customer's requirements.
- Define the NWT's requirements.
- Determine how compliance to the requirements will be measured.
- Define acceptable performance levels (i.e., performance standards).
- Define the customer-feedback process.

Phase 4 is divided into seven steps:

1. Select the critical process.
2. Identify customer(s) for each output.
3. Define customer requirements.
4. Define measurements.
5. Review with customers.
6. Define feedback procedure.
7. Reconcile customer requirements with mission and processes.

Phase 5—Analyze the Process's Efficiency

For each major process, the NWT must define and understand the tasks that make up the process by analyzing each major process for its value-added content. This can be accomplished by flowcharting the process and each major activity for its value-added content and collecting efficiency information related to each task and the total process. Typical information that would be collected includes:

- Cycle time
- Processing time
- Cost
- Rework rates
- Items processed per time period

Using this information, the NWT will establish efficiency measurements and performance targets for each efficiency measurement.

Phase 5 is divided into six steps:

1. Define efficiency measurements.
2. Understand the current process.
3. Define data reporting systems.
4. Define performance requirements.
5. Approve performance standards.
6. Establish a performance board.

Phase 6—Develop Supplier Partnerships

Using the flowcharts generated in phase 5, the NWT identifies the suppliers that provide input into the major processes. This phase uses the same approach discussed in phase 4 but turns the customer-supplier relationship around. In phase 6, the area is told to view itself in the role of the customer. The organizations that are providing the inputs to the NWTs are called internal or external suppliers. The area meets with its suppliers to develop agreed-upon requirements. As a result of these negotiations, a supplier specification is prepared, which includes a measurement system, performance standards, and feedback system for each input.

This completes the customer-supplier chain for the area, as shown in figure 1.2 in chapter 1.

What is a supplier? There are different kinds, and they can have different priorities and controls applied to them.

A *supplier* is an organization that provides a product (i.e., input) to the customer. (Source: ISO 8402.)

Internal suppliers are areas within an organizational structure that provide input into other areas within the same organizational structure.

External suppliers are suppliers that aren't part of the customer's organizational structure.

Phase 6 is divided into five steps:

1. Identify supplier(s).
2. Define requirements.
3. Define measurements and performance standards.
4. Define feedback procedure.
5. Obtain supplier agreement.

Phase 7—Performance Improvement

The continuous improvement phase should begin after a process has been defined and the related measurements put in place.

During phase 7, the NWT switches into problem-solving and error-prevention modes of operation. The measurement system should now be used to set challenging improvement targets, and the NWT should be trained to solve problems and take advantage of improvement opportunities. The individual efficiency and effectiveness measurements are combined into a single performance index for the area. Typically the area's key measurement graphs will be posted and updated regularly.

During phase 7, management should show its appreciation to the NWT, individuals who expended exceptional effort during the AAA project, and those who implemented major improvements.

Phase 7 is divided into eight steps:

1. Set up the reporting systems.
2. Identify the processes to be improved.
3. Install temporary protection, if needed.
4. Identify measurements or tasks to be improved.
5. Find best-value solutions.
6. Implement solutions.
7. Remove temporary protection, if installed.
8. Prevent problems from recurring.

For more information on AAA, see my book, *Area Activity Analysis* (McGraw-Hill, 1998).

THE OPPORTUNITY CYCLE

Let's change the way we look at problems. We should think about each problem we face as an opportunity to contribute to making the organization more successful. As these opportunities arise, we need a systematic way of addressing them so that they are not just put to bed, but ended. If you put a problem to bed, it can and will get up some time in the future to cause the organization more disruptions. It may be next week, or next month, or next year, or perhaps in five years, but it will come back unless the process that allowed the problem to occur initially is error-proofed. When you have error-proofed the process that allowed the problem to occur, then and only then have you ended the problem. That's what the opportunity cycle is all about. (See figure 3.2.)

When you investigate each problem, go through the six distinct phases indicated in figure 3.2. Each phase contains a number of individual activities. The total cycle consists of 25 different activities.

■ Phase 1: Opportunity selection
　□ Activity 1: Listing the problems

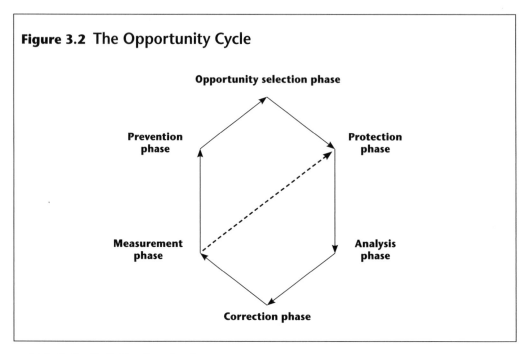

Figure 3.2 The Opportunity Cycle

☐ Activity 2: Collecting the data
☐ Activity 3: Verifying the problems
☐ Activity 4: Prioritizing the problems
☐ Activity 5: Selecting the problems
☐ Activity 6: Defining the problems

■ Phase 2: Protection
☐ Activity 7: Taking action to protect the customer
☐ Activity 8: Verifying the effectiveness of the action taken

■ Phase 3: Analysis
☐ Activity 9: Collecting problem symptoms
☐ Activity 10: Validating the problem
☐ Activity 11: Separating cause and effect
☐ Activity 12: Defining the root cause

■ Phase 4: Correction
☐ Activity 13: Developing alternative solutions
☐ Activity 14: Selecting the best solution
☐ Activity 15: Developing an implementation plan

☐ Activity 16: Conducting a pilot run
☐ Activity 17: Presenting the solution for approval

■ Phase 5: Measurement
☐ Activity 18: Implementing the approved plan
☐ Activity 19: Measuring cost and impact
☐ Activity 20: Removing the protective action installed during phase 2

■ Phase 6: Prevention
☐ Activity 21: Applying solution to similar activities
☐ Activity 22: Defining and correcting the basic process problem
☐ Activity 23: Changing the process documentation to prevent recurrence
☐ Activity 24: Providing proper training
☐ Activity 25: Return to phase 1, activity 1

Following these six phases (or a similar process) makes team members' lives much easier. Unfortunately, the more experienced the teams become, the more likely they are to take shortcuts. Process shortcuts have led to the demise of more teams than can be counted. When a team elects to circumvent the correct problem-solving process, it automatically reduces its ability to function in a continuous improvement environment. The team might ultimately succeed, but it will be by accident, not by design.

TEAM MICRO-LEVEL APPROACHES TO PROCESS MANAGEMENT

Although the AAA methodology is the best approach to getting a team involved in continuously improving the organization's processes, other teams can also be effectively used:

■ *Quality control circles.* These teams are often used to empower employees to define improvement opportunities and to solve them.
■ *Task teams.* These teams are used when management identifies an improvement opportunity and assigns employees to improve the condition.
■ *Task forces.* These teams are used when a major improvement opportunity is defined by management that must be addressed immediately.
■ *Autonomous work teams/self-managed work teams.* These teams are used when a NWT and the measurement system have developed to a point where the employees can manage themselves. They select the improvement opportunities they will work on.

DEPARTMENTAL MICRO-LEVEL APPROACH TO PROCESS MANAGEMENT

Throughout the organization there are departments formed to continuously improve processes. For example, manufacturing engineering is continuously working to improve the manufacturing process. Product engineering's role, after a design is released, is to continuously improve it. Quality assurance's role is to reduce waste. The human resources department is always looking for ways to improve the reward-and-recognition system.

All organizations spend a large part of their yearly budgets on resources intended to continuously improve their processes. Management has the right to expect a minimum of a 10-percent annual reduction in cost and cycle time as a result of these continuous improvement efforts.

FAST-ACTION SOLUTION TEAMS

Fast action solution teams (FAST) are an effective way to obtain corrective action, focused at a specific subprocess or activity. These teams are usually headed by one or two members of the process improvement team. This approach is designed to pick the "low-hanging fruit," i.e., the easy-to-take-advantage-of opportunities related to a subprocess or activity. FAST includes the following steps:

1. The FAST leaders identify a subprocess or activity that has many problems or numerous opportunities for improvement.
2. They identify a manager who has the authority to authorize changes to the subprocess or activity and ask him or her to sponsor the activity. The manager must understand that at the end of the two-day session, he or she will accept or reject the suggested improvements. The sponsor does not have the luxury of postponing the decision.
3. The FAST leaders develop a flowchart of the subprocess or activity and a FAST mission statement that is approved by the FAST sponsor.
4. A one- or two-day meeting is held with key people involved in the subprocess or activity. Other key support people are often invited as well. The meeting is run continuously for both days. The ground rules for this meeting are:
   - Only discuss problems or improvement opportunities related to the assigned area.
   - All suggestions must be able to be implemented by the people who make up the FAST.
   - All suggestions should be capable of being implemented within 90 days.
   - All suggestions should result in measurable improvements.
   - All suggestions should have a FAST member assigned to them who has agreed to be responsible for implementing the suggestion.

5. At the end of the two-day session, the FAST presents its findings to its management sponsor, and recommended actions are accepted or rejected.
6. The FAST leaders prepare minutes of the FAST activities that include an implementation schedule of the approved suggestions.
7. The FAST leaders and the management sponsor track the action items to ensure that they are implemented as scheduled.

Present-State   Future-State

FAST improvement to subprocesses or activities has been used extensively by many organizations, including Ford and General Electric, both of which have run literally hundreds of FAST analyses. Another name for the FAST methodology is Express. GE calls it Workout.

The illustration above shows a roller skate that has gone through the continuous improvement process.

INDIVIDUALS CAN IMPROVE THEIR PROCESSES

You don't need teams to improve processes. Each employee can do much to better the processes in which he or she is involved. Simply giving individuals the responsibility to improve the way they work leads to a marvelous transformation throughout the organization.

SUGGESTIONS FOR MICRO-LEVEL PROCESS MANAGEMENT

It's human nature to complain. Ask your employees what is wrong, and they will tell you—if they aren't afraid of you and what will happen to them if they speak up. William Shakespeare said, "Language developed because of our deep inner need to complain." Process management should transform these complaints into creative solutions suggested by the person who made the complaint. Management needs people to offer solutions, not problems. Management must help employees develop their ideas, not kill the ideas. 3M's eleventh commandment is, "Thou shalt not kill an idea."

The problem is getting employees to convert their complaints into useable ideas. The solution requires management to create an environment where it's OK to think. When IBM was truly great, under the leadership of Thomas J. Watson Sr., its motto was just one word: Think!

An important part of developing a creative, thinking environment within an organization is the open sharing of ideas. To accomplish this, 3M, for example, has "innovation fairs" to exhibit its employees' new ideas.

FORMAL SUGGESTION SYSTEMS

Suggestion systems are a proven, effective method of profiting from your employees' creative abilities. A formal suggestion system allows employees to submit their ideas for evaluation and implementation, even when their job descriptions don't include generating such ideas. For example, an assembly worker would not be responsible for designing assembly fixtures. However, if the worker had an idea about how to improve a fixture, that would be an appropriate idea for a formal suggestion system.

"When we [by suggestions] can reduce the cost of producing the product, we are willing to share that gain with our people on what we believe is a fair and equitable basis. Again, this further reflects the broader value of an idea unleashed."
—Joe Magliochetti
CEO, Dana Corp.

The suggestion system is a U.S. concept started in 1896 by National Cash Register Co. A typical formal suggestion system requires the employee to document his or her ideas for improvement and submit them to a central suggestion department that's responsible for coordinating and evaluating the ideas. The suggestion department is required to report back to the employee about the status of his or her idea. If the suggestion is accepted by the evaluation area, the evaluator would determine the tangible savings that will result from the idea, and a portion of them would be given to the suggester. This can potentially generate thousands of dollars of additional income for an employee during a year.

There are two types of employee suggestion systems:

- Suggestions that are outside of the individual's job description. For example, a secretary who suggests the use of a different printer because it will improve production. These are the classic suggestion systems.

- Suggestions that the employee is responsible for developing, i.e., suggestions that are part of his or her job description to develop (frequently called job improvement programs). For example, product engineers changing a design that was assigned to them.

Classic Suggestion Systems

The classic suggestion system was designed to pay employees for their ideas that are outside of their job description. The key elements of this type of suggestion system are:

■ The suggestion must not be part of the suggester's responsibility.

■ The suggestion does not have to be implemented to be considered.

■ The suggester shares in the savings resulting from the suggestion.

■ The suggestion can't be predated by activities or plans already underway.

How does the suggestion system work? It offers the person closest to the work activity the opportunity to suggest improvements. This results in more effective utilization of assets, increased productivity, waste reduction, lower product costs, and improved quality.

Paul Revere Insurance Co. employees submitted 20,000 suggestions during the first three years of its improvement process. The suggestions were a major contributor to the organization's improved performance, leading to:

■ A 200-percent increase in income with no additional staff

■ The organization moving from No. 2 to No. 1 in its field of insurance

Suggestion Rewards

IBM's suggestion system pays its employees 25 percent of the net savings for the first two years after the suggestion is implemented with a minimum reward of $50 and a maximum of $100,000. Eli Lilly also rewards its employees 25 percent of the net savings, but the national average for all organizations in the United States is 17 percent.

> **"A new idea, like a human being, has a life cycle. It is born. If properly nurtured, it grows. When it matures, it becomes a productive member of society."**
> **—Frank K. Sonnenberg**
> *It's A Great Idea, But . . .*

Japan's Suggestion System

During the 1950s the suggestion system became a main contributor to Japan's continuous improvement efforts. Toyota's suggestion system manual states: "The system came to Toyota from the United States back in 1951, when Toyota was still a newcomer in the automotive industry. Two Toyota officials traveled to the United States to study modern management methods, and at Ford Motor they saw a suggestion system being used that inspired them to try a similar system at Toyota." Toyota management feels that improvements and suggestions by team members are the cornerstone of Toyota's success.

Suggestion systems became a main staple of the Japanese continuous improvement process, far surpassing the benefits the country received from the quality control circle concept. The Japanese Suggestion Association reported that, "As viewed from the relationship with small group activities, which is the nucleus of the suggestion activities, fifty times as many suggestions are made for every solution of one problem by a quality control circle."

The typical Japanese suggestion system places much less emphasis on the monetary savings per suggestion and much more emphasis on submitting many suggestions. The system is not a passive one that waits for suggestions to come from employees. It's an active system that educates, promotes, and gives targets for suggestions. Japan's suggestion system started by building into the Japanese worker the habit of making suggestions. This includes training people to be effective at generating new ideas and documenting them. Targets are established for the number of suggestions per employee, and lists of participants and nonparticipants are published. The objective is to encourage every person to become an active participant in the suggestion system. Major organizations throughout Japan have been successful in this regard. This has resulted in millions of suggestions being submitted each year—an average of 17 suggestions per participant per year. On an average, more than 90 percent of all the suggestions submitted in Japan are implemented.

The Japanese suggestion system, with its focus on quantity of suggestions and 100-percent participation, resulted in many ideas that were directly related to employees' environments and jobs. The suggestions could be implemented by the employees who made them, at little cost, and requiring only the approval of the employee's manager. As a result, the system was modified to allow suggestions to be implemented without going through a suggestion department. It also resulted in a greatly reduced cash reward system for the employees. In Japan the focus is not on the cash rewards but on meeting committed quantities of suggestions.

Problems With U.S. Suggestion Systems

The major reasons that suggestion systems aren't as effective as they should be in the United States include:

- Lack of management involvement
- Long evaluation cycles
- Lack of goal setting
- Lack of recognition

The quantity of employee suggestions is directly proportional to the manager's interest in the suggestion process. Japanese suggestion systems are very successful because everyone commits to them. Each department should set a target for the number of suggestions that it will submit every three months. This helps make the suggestion system a challenge for the department and its members.

Job Improvement Program

The second type of suggestion system relates to ideas that are part of the individual's job description. The job improvement program provides a way for organizations to encourage employees to use their creativity and receive recognition for creative accomplishments that they implemented within their area of job responsibilities—accomplishments that aren't eligible for suggestion awards. All items that are candidates for job improvement programs should be implemented before the job improvement form is submitted. Because job improvement is a responsibility of all employees, the department manager is required to submit a job improvement commitment for the coming year and measure himself or herself and the department against these goals. For example, a typical commitment would be to record a minimum of $500,000 savings during the next twelve months and have 100 percent of the employees participating by submitting a minimum of one job improvement idea. Often this is carried forward and included on the individual's performance plan for the coming year.

Typically job improvement program results become part of the individual's personnel file, showing his or her major contributions to the organization. These creativity performance data are important considerations when an individual is being considered for a promotion or transferred to a new assignment. At IBM, each month the individuals who recorded the most savings from each function within their particular locations were invited to participate in a luncheon with the location managers. There, the employee received a token gift, and each individual explained to the group what he or she did to improve the organization's performance. Often this would be the only time that the employee was able to present his or her contribution to that level of management.

Other organizations give points for each improvement—the bigger the savings, the more points the individual receives. At the end of the year, a drawing is held where prizes are given out. The number of points an individual has accumulated during the year determines the number of chances that the individual has to win. Actual examples of some of these prizes include cars, all-expense-paid vacations for two to Tahiti, new computers, and a two-week Caribbean cruise for two. Of course, other less expensive prizes are also given out. The average prize is less than $200.

The job improvement program can also provide management with information that leads to the employee receiving one of the major organizational awards at a later date. A typical example of a job improvement award is a reserved parking space for one month with the employee's name prominently displayed.

Documented Ideas Program (Quick and Easy *Kaizen*)

> "Suggestions are a lot like a baseball game. The home run hitters get all the press, but it's the guys who hit the singles and doubles that win the game."
>
> —Anonymous

The first year that Technicolor Detroit started to use quick and easy *kaizen* it received 1,320 suggestions in just one month. This compares to only thirteen suggestions for the previous twelve months.

The documented ideas program, or as Norman Bodek (the man who brought lean manufacturing to the United States) calls it, "quick and easy *kaizen*," is a combination of the U.S. job improvement program and the Japanese suggestion system. These ideas are usually simple to implement, at little or no cost. They relate to the individual's job and the surrounding area. In his book *Quick and Easy Kaizen* (PCS Press, 2001), Bodek says, "I know that every worker is filled with unlimited ideas on how to improve their job and the environment around them, but unfortunately, hardly ever does anyone ask you for your ideas." He also points out that, "At Dana Corp. they receive an average of two implemented ideas per month per employee—twenty-four implemented ideas per year." Dana Corp. had two million ideas submitted last year, and 80 percent of them were implemented.

Bodek suggests that everyone ask the following questions:

- How would you improve customer service?
- Are there any potential safety problems lurking around you, like a box ready to fall?
- Can you find every tool in thirty seconds?
- Can you do something to make sure that you will not spill something on your desk?
- Can you suggest something that will help you save some time?
- Is your work area sparkling clean and neat?
- Do you have a smile or a frown on your face?
- Are your work instructions right in front of you, and are they easy to read and understand?

The primary purpose of this approach is to help an organization generate a lot of improvement ideas and to empower its employees to make decisions and install their ideas themselves or with the help and/or cooperation of other team members.

The documented ideas program consists of four basic activities:

- Training employees to recognize simple improvement opportunities and how to correct them. (For example, rearranging the layout of the individual's desk.)
- Empowering employees to make changes to their work that improves their performance without having a negative effect on other people.
- Documenting their improvement ideas (after they have been implemented) on a simple form that contains:

□ The situation before implementation

□ The situation after implementation

□ The effects of implementation

■ Sharing the idea and results with the rest of the organization.

> "It's important to note that the people who have the idea at organizations like Toyota and Dana in most cases are the ones who implement the idea."
>
> —HJH

In companies like Toyota Motor Co., individual work groups set objectives for the number of ideas that will be generated by the group for each year. These commitments to the corporation are then tracked and visually displayed in the work areas. As a result, Toyota receives approximately seventy improvement ideas in writing per employee per year. Compare this to the United States, where the average idea per employee is one every seven years. Joe Magliochetti, chairman and CEO of Dana Corp., stated, "We find that the people who are most prolific in their ideas and in their involvement are the most satisfied as well." When questioned about the cost of running a quick and easy *kaizen* process, he stated, "While these programs do require investment, this expense pales in comparison to the cost of not pursuing such a course."

Suggestions don't have to be breakthrough concepts. These programs thrive on simple improvement ideas. In *Quick and Easy Kaizen* Norman Bodek provides many simple examples. Two of these are:

■ "At Technicolor's DVD packaging, one employee spent all his time closing boxes. He came up with an idea of using two pieces of wood covered with cardboard to close the box covers."

■ "At Possis Medical in Minneapolis the employees had a hard time finding the remote control for the LCD. An employee suggested that two velcro strips be used to hold it on the unit when it was not in use."

> **"We are always looking for small, incremental improvements. We always want to challenge the status quo."**
>
> **—Brian Bergsteinsson
> Vice president and general
> manager, Lexus Group**

Angel's Advocate

Managers throughout the years have played the role of the devil's advocate. Whenever an employee brings an idea to the manager, he or she points out all the possible things that could go wrong. Because managers have a bigger picture of the total organization, they feel that they have the responsibility to point out the negative effect an idea could have on the organization. This approach protects the organization from being bombarded with many ideas that are of no value, but it also has the opposite effect—of overwhelming employees

"It was just an old block of stone setting in the sun until Michelangelo walked by and saw David inside waiting to be released."

—Anonymous

with obstacles to making suggestions. After going through this cycle two or three times, the employee gives up, feeling that the effort isn't worthwhile. As a result, good ideas are discarded or not even created. Management's role in the creative process has to change. Instead of being a devil's advocate, a manager must become an angel's advocate. An angel's advocate helps employees develop their ideas and provides employees with positive feedback and suggestions on how to improve on them. Management should make employees feel that each idea, which they just gave birth to, is important to the organization and that they are contributing in a positive way. Today there is no place for a devil's advocate in the organization. Everyone must be an angel's advocate.

CHAPTER IV

THE MACRO-LEVEL APPROACH
TO PROCESS MANAGEMENT

"Sometimes continuous improvement is just not enough."
—HJH

In 1926 Henry Ford and his team designed a process that allowed them to produce a car in four days, beginning with iron ore as it came out of the mines and ending with an assembled and tested car, ready to be delivered to the customer. Today's benchmark for that cycle is more than 93 days—20 times longer. This benchmark indicates how much improvement is possible in most organizations.

The macro-level approach focuses on the major processes that drive organizations, those considered to be core capabilities and competencies. Most manufacturing processes are included in this category, but the macro-level approach isn't limited to manufacturing processes. Today, the processes that involve and support the knowledge worker are often more important than manufacturing processes.

Managing macro-level processes—called Harrington's Fine Methodology—contains three phases:

- Phase 1—Define (redefine) the process
- Phase 2—Confine the process
- Phase 3—Refine the process

PHASE 1—DEFINE (REDEFINE) THE PROCESS

If this is a new process, one that doesn't currently exist, you will be defining it. If it is a process that already exists, you will be redefining it.

During phase 1 the organization must identify the processes that are managed at the macro-level and understand how they fit into the organization's structure. Phase 1 contains eight steps:

> **"Downsizing has turned out to be something that surgeons for centuries have warned against: amputation before diagnosis. The result is always a casualty."**
> **—Peter Drucker**
> **Author, management consultant, and university professor**

1. Identify the macro-level processes.
2. Identify the process owners.
3. Identify the process improvement team.
4. Prepare a process mission statement.
5. Box in the process.
6. Define the process's customer(s) and related measurements.
7. Define the process's supplier(s) and related measurements.
8. Define the process efficiency measurements.

Identify the Macro-Level Processes

In chapter 1 we defined a way to identify the major processes within the organization. The macro-level approach focuses its efforts on these cross-functional major processes.

Trying to manage all major processes often creates problems because of the initial effort required to define and bring them under control, especially if the organization doesn't already have a strong process focus. The organization should prioritize its list of macro processes and select no more than twelve to apply process management to initially. As a process completes its phase 2 activities, an additional process should be added to the list until all the priority processes have been addressed.

> **"Identify an opportunity that provides not only financial and customer benefits, but reduces the pain and grief for those involved in running the process day to day."**
> **—Ian J. May**
> **CEO, Siemens**

A number of factors should be considered at this point. Is there a need to redesign or reengineer any of the processes? Would a more conservative, continuous improvement approach be adequate? To determine if a major process should be redesigned or reengineered, consider the following issues about each of the macro processes.

- Customer impact—How much does the customer care?
- Changeability index—Can it be fixed?
- Performance status—How damaged is it?
- Business impact—How important is it to the business?
- Work impact—How many resources does it consume?
- Technical status—How current is the process technology?
- Change status—What projects are already underway to change the process?

After considering these factors, most organizations realize that some of their major processes must undergo a rapid transformation. If the improvement requires that cost and cycle time be reduced by 30 to 60 percent, the redesign methodology is the best option. If a more aggressive improvement of 60 to 90 percent is needed, then the reengineering approach should be used. If a 5 to 15 percent improvement per year is acceptable, a continuous improvement approach should be used.

Major processes that are scheduled for process redesign, reengineering, or the addition of a major new software system shouldn't be included in the list for process management because they will become part of a separate project. Once they have completed their transformation, they will be added to the macro-level process list.

For more information on selecting processes for reengineering or redesign, see my book *Business Process Improvement* (McGraw-Hill, 1991).

Identify Process Owners

Most major processes flow across organizations in chimneys, commonly called functions (e.g., production control, development, sales, manufacturing, and marketing). As a result, no one is responsible for the overall effectiveness and efficiency of the major processes. (See figure 4.1)

In many processes major problems occur at the points where outputs move from one function to another. These handoff points typically represent voids or overlaps in the process. Each function is trying to optimize the resources involved in its part of the process. This often results in increased cost in other functions. As a result, it's important that each of the major processes has a process owner assigned to it. (A process owner is sometimes called a process champion because the organization wants *all* of its employees involved in the process to consider themselves process owners.)

John Akers, former CEO of IBM, stated, "In a large and complex organization like ours, the need is exponentially greater for managers to own their processes." Process owners are

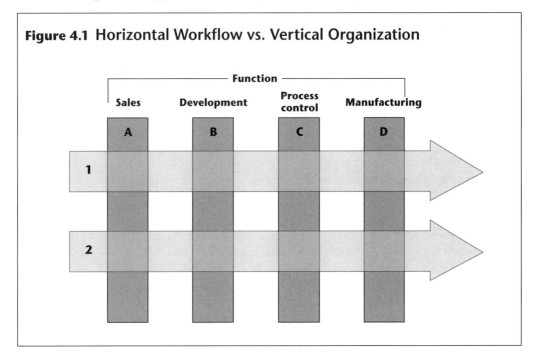

Figure 4.1 Horizontal Workflow vs. Vertical Organization

responsible for improving the assigned process to the point that it represents best-of-breed status. They must then keep it at that level.

In selecting a process owner, ask the following questions:

- Who has the most resources consumed by the process?
- Who spends the most time working within the process?
- Who's subjected to the largest amount of difficulty as a result of firefighting, complaints, or inefficiencies in the process?
- Who will receive the most credit if the process is managed well?
- Who gains the most if things go well?
- Who has the ability to effect change in the process?

Once you've answered these questions and identified particular individuals within the organization, you'll have a list of people who would be good candidates to manage the process. It's important that the process owner operates at a high enough level in the organization to:

- Identify the effect of new business direction on the process
- Influence change in policies and procedures affecting the process
- Commit to a plan and implement change
- Monitor the effectiveness and efficiency of the process

Another important consideration in the selection of a process owner is his or her personal traits. He or she should:

- Be perceived as highly credible
- Have the ability to inspire others
- Be a skilled negotiator
- Be willing to embrace change
- Be able to overcome roadblocks
- Be a visionary
- Be willing to take risks
- Be creative
- Enjoy being measured based upon results

Select process owners carefully because they will have a major effect on the way your processes are managed and, by extension, the overall performance of the organization.

An example of a good process owner is Linda Sanford, a senior vice president for IBM, who led a team responsible for taking $5 billion out of IBM's supply chain.

Identify the Process Improvement Team

Once the process owner is identified, he or she will define the beginning and end boundaries of the process. The process owner should make a box diagram of the process flow as it moves from department to department. Considering this process flow diagram, the process owner will then meet with managers in the related departments and invite each of them to assign an employee to represent the departments on the process improvement team (PIT). The selected department representatives should have:

- The authority to commit the department's resources
- Time to participate and implement the process management structure
- Time to follow up on assignments given out during process meetings
- Practical knowledge of the process as it relates to their departments
- Credibility with the other PIT members
- A desire to see the process improve
- A willingness to embrace and lead change
- A vested interest in the process

Members of the PIT should have a background in basic team operation and problem-solving techniques. They should have previous training in:

- Team processes
- Brainstorming
- Check sheets
- Graphs
- Histograms (frequency distributions)
- Pareto diagrams
- Scatter diagrams
- Nominal group techniques
- Delphi narrowing techniques
- Force field analysis
- Cause-and-effect diagrams
- Mind maps
- Statistical process control

If they haven't been trained in these areas, they should familiarize themselves with all of these basic tools early in the process. In addition to these basic tools, the PIT will be using the twelve basic business process improvement tools discussed in chapter 2.

As well as the twelve basic business process improvement tools, the twelve sophisticated tools discussed in chapter 2 and used only on special occasions will prove helpful.

Typically, the PIT is introduced to the basic and sophisticated business process improvement tools on a need-to-know basis. Just-in-time training that is immediately applied to the process is far more effective than classroom training.

Prepare a Process Mission Statement

One of the first things the PIT does is prepare a mission statement for the process. This statement defines what the process is intended to accomplish. A good mission statement should:

- Be short (no more than five sentences)
- Define the scope of the process
- State what must be accomplished
- Include, as appropriate, key process objectives and/or measurements

Box in the Process

The PIT will then review the beginning and end boundaries that were set by the process owner and ensure that they are correct. The PIT will also establish upper and lower boundaries. This is called "boxing in the process." Figure 4.2 shows an example of a boxed-in process for a steak barbecue.

Upper boundaries define items that enter the process between the beginning and end points. For example, your process might require funds to purchase an item, but the process of acquiring the funds should be considered as outside of this specific macro process. In this case, the money would come into the upper boundaries, but the process of acquiring the money would be outside of the scope of the process you are managing. Lower boundaries, on the other hand, are items that leave the process between the beginning and end boundaries. For example, you might send a purchase order to the purchasing department to buy equipment for the process, but you shouldn't include the equipment negotiation and order cycle as part of your process.

Boxing in the process provides a clear picture of what is contained within the process. It's an important step in looking at the organization's total process management activities. As individual boxes are completed, they help tie the overall business process together, providing a complete picture of the systems within the organization.

Define Customers and Their Related Measurements

The PIT should define who will receive the outputs from the process and document an agreement of what an acceptable output is. It's often necessary to look beyond the immediate recipient of the process output. Your customer's customers might have additional special requirements. For example, when production control releases a production order to manufacturing, it doesn't care where the product will be shipped. However, when the product has completed the manufacturing cycle and has been delivered to the shipping

Figure 4.2 Boxing in the Steak BBQ Process

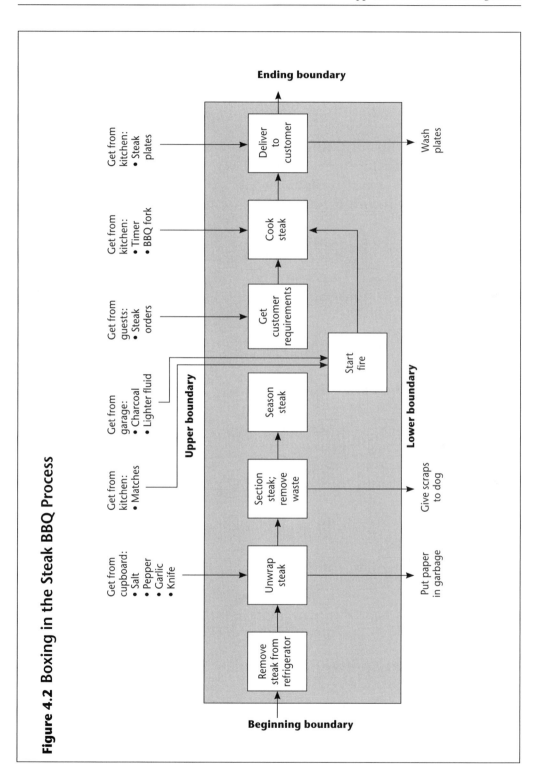

area, the customer's name, address, and promised delivery date are crucial information that shipping must have.

The primary measure of output from a process is effectiveness, which goes far beyond just quality. Effectiveness is having the right output at the right place at the right time at the right price. Effectiveness affects the customer.

Define the Suppliers and Related Measurements

Just as it's necessary to have the process output requirements defined and documented, it's equally important to communicate the process input requirements in a document that both suppliers and the process owner have signed off on.

Define the Process's Efficiency Measurements

Efficiency is defined as the extent to which resources are maximized and/or wasted in converting the process inputs into process outputs. Productivity is a measure of efficiency. Typical efficiency-type measures would be percent of time spent in rework, cost per order processed, maximum time from entry into the process to completion of the process (i.e., cycle time).

PHASE 2—CONFINE THE PROCESS

In this phase the process improvement team will qualify the process. They will gain a detailed understanding of the process and what it's capable of performing. This phase involves the following steps:

1. Prepare process flowcharts.
2. Perform a process walkthrough.
3. Evaluate the process's paperwork.
4. Characterize the process's activities.
5. Install the measurement (control) systems.
6. Qualify the process.

For those processes that will be reengineered, redesigned, or have major new software programs installed, the PIT should stop after step three and go directly to phase 3.

Prepare Process Flowcharts

The PIT should make a flowchart of the process down to the activity level. There are six basic types of flowchart techniques that should be considered:

- Block diagrams, which provide a quick overall view of the process
- The American National Standards Institute flowcharts, which analyze the detailed interrelationships of a process

- Functional flowcharts, which depict the process flow between organizations and areas
- Graphic flowcharts, which illustrate the process flow between locations
- Communication flowcharts, which portray how communication flows between organizations or activities
- Process knowledge maps, which visually display knowledge within the context of a business process, show how knowledge should be used within the process, and the sources of this knowledge.

For most processes, the team will start with a simple block diagram and then detail it using a functional flowchart. Techniques like communication flowcharting or graphic flowcharting are most effective when used in conjunction with a process improvement effort. The PIT should use a flowcharting software package to accomplish this task. In some cases the process flowcharts (or process maps) are converted into simulation models. This is an effective way to understand how well the process will function over time and under stress. Some of the organizations that supply workflow process management software are:

- Docucorp International Inc.
- Document Imaging Solutions Inc.
- DST Technologies Inc.
- Edge Software
- eiStream Inc.
- Entopia Inc.
- Exact Software North America
- Fast Search & Transfer (FAST)
- FileNet Corp.
- Hyland Software Inc.
- Identitech Inc.
- InSystems Corp.
- Integrify
- Kamoon Inc.
- KMtechnologies Inc.
- LEGATO Software
- Liberty IMS
- Open Text Corp.
- RedDot Solutions
- SiteScape Inc.
- Smead
- Stellent Inc.
- SupportSoft

> **"Though this be madness, yet there is method in it."**
> **—William Shakespeare**
> *Hamlet*

- TimeVision Inc.
- TOWER Software
- Ultimus

For more information on flowcharting, see my book, *Business Process Improvement* (McGraw-Hill, 1991). For information on simulation modeling, see my book, *Simulation Modeling Methods* (McGraw-Hill, 2000.)

Knowledge maps are an important means to understanding major processes and improving their performance. French Caldwell of Gartner Group stated, "There will be an increased emphasis during the next few years on taxonomies, ontologies, and knowledge." Any type of knowledge that drives the process or results from executing the process can be mapped. This includes tacit (i.e., soft) knowledge or explicit (i.e., hard) knowledge.

Perform a Process Walkthrough

Once the flowchart is completed, the PIT should validate the flowchart and add additional information to it. Examples include:

- Cycle time
- Processing time
- Cost
- Documents used
- Problems related to the process
- Suggested improvements

This type of data can be effectively added to the flowchart if the PIT is using a software product. To manage it by hand often becomes cumbersome.

To collect this data, the PIT must conduct a process walkthrough. The PIT will start with the end customer and follow the process map backward to its beginning input point. This allows the PIT to meet with each activity's customer before reviewing the activity. The process walkthrough should always be conducted in the area where the work is being performed, not in a conference room. The PIT should meet with the people doing the work, not with their manager. Prior to reviewing an activity, the PIT should be supplied with all related paperwork. This will allow team members to become familiar with the activity so they can ask intelligent questions and verify that employees are following their instructions. Also, before conducting a process walkthrough, a process walkthrough questionnaire should be prepared. Typical questions include:

- What are the required inputs?
- How are you trained?
- What do you do?
- How do you know your output is good?

- What feedback do you receive?
- Who are your customers?
- What keeps you from doing error-free work?
- What can be done to make your job easier?
- How do you let your suppliers know how well they are performing?
- How is your output used?
- What happens if you don't do the job?
- Have you reviewed your job description?
- What would happen if each of your suppliers stopped providing you with input?
- What would you change if you were a manager?

One of the more difficult pieces of information to collect is cycle time. This is particularly true when a process is in the startup stage. But don't become discouraged if you have problems with cycle-time estimates. They are extremely important and often are as much as 100 times greater than processing time. The best way to obtain a good estimate is to start an item at the beginning of the process and measure the time it takes to complete the process cycle. This is usually more accurate than trying to measure the actual cycle times between each activity and adding them together.

Evaluate the Process's Paperwork

After completing the process walkthrough, the PIT is in an excellent position to evaluate the paperwork used to control the process. Typical paperwork that's evaluated includes:

- Routings
- Training materials
- Setup documents
- Specifications
- Inspection procedures
- Operating documents
- Maintenance documents
- Operating procedures
- Corrective action procedures
- Packaging and shipping documents
- Safety and security procedures

Characterize the Process's Activities

The PIT must look at each activity to determine if it's capable of meeting its output requirements at an acceptable level. The acceptable level should be zero errors. However, humans and equipment can't perform error-free for an indefinite period of time. As a result, many organizations have accepted a general standard called six sigma, or 3.4

defects per million items processed. The problem with setting a six sigma standard is the difficulty of knowing if the activity is meeting the standard. This is where statisticians are helpful. They have observed that variation normally occurs in a set pattern called a normal frequency distribution, sometimes also called a histogram or normal distribution. (See figure 4.3.)

Statisticians have developed a formula that defines a histogram that reflects the total population using a relatively small sample of items. This technique makes use of standard deviation, which measures data variation. Standard deviation is represented by the Greek letter sigma (σ). Plus or minus 1 sigma from the mean of the data is equal to 68.26 percent of the total population. (Mean is defined as the average of the data collected.) At plus or minus three sigma, 99.73 percent of all the population should fall within this range. Be aware that this is a simplified explanation of the use of histograms and sigma. This is the simplest of all the histograms to work with, but in business processes, the result is often an abnormal distribution. In these cases the math is a little more complex, but as luck would have it, computer programs now take care of most of the statistical calculations, so anyone can perform the analysis.

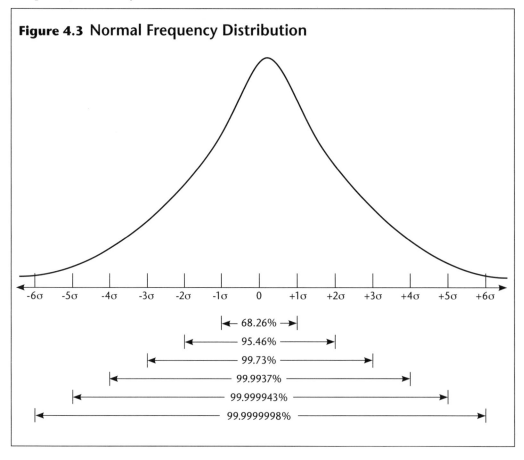

Figure 4.3 Normal Frequency Distribution

For a more thorough explanation, see my book, *Statistical Analysis Simplified* (McGraw-Hill, 1998).

Once the PIT has calculated sigma for an activity, it can compare the calculated deviation to the requirements to determine if the process is capable of meeting the specified requirements at that specific time and under those conditions. This is called process capability (Cp). When the PIT takes into consideration how the process data are centralized around the requirements' midpoint and other factors that could cause variation that were not considered when running the sample (e.g., variation in employee[s], materials, setups, temperature, etc.), it is called Cpk. We consider a Cpk of 1.4 good enough to certify most activities. Cpk is calculated by taking the plus or minus three sigma spread (or 99.7 percent of the total population), as statistically estimated when all the variables are considered, and dividing it into allowable or specified acceptable variations. For example, if allowable process time for an order in Organization X is three hours (plus or minus fifteen minutes) and the plus or minus three-sigma processing time points are two hours and fifty minutes to three hours and ten minutes, Cpk is calculated in this way:

$$Cpk = \text{allowable variation} = 2{:}45 - 3{:}15 = 30 \text{ minutes} = 1.5$$
$$\pm 3\sigma = 2{:}50 - 3{:}10$$
$$20 \; Cpk = 1.5$$

Again, this is a very simplified definition of Cpk.

During the 1980s, IBM's standard for inspection and test activities was a Cpk of 1.4 for the combination of all measurements at that inspection or test operation. With an average of seven measurements at each operation, that was 500 percent more stringent than today's six sigma standard of 1.5 for each opportunity.

For a Cpk of 1.0 or less, inspection procedures should be put in place to ensure that defective items are not delivered to the customer.

Install the Measurement (Control) Systems

One of the biggest problems facing management is providing an efficient measurement system for today's knowledge worker. The importance of good feedback can't be overestimated.

I once had an employee tell me, "If management doesn't measure it, it's not important." This probably isn't true, but we do know that management measures the things that are important to it (e.g., return on investment, cost for unit processed, dollars of sales, stock prices, etc.).

"What gets measured, gets done."
—Anonymous

Too often, measurements are used to punish employees. Measurements should be used to help everyone improve. Measurements also provide an excellent recognition system for employees who are excelling at their jobs. The only person who doesn't want to be measured is the poor performer.

Why is it that employees will complain when the office temperature gets up to 80 degrees but will take off early to go play five sets of tennis in 90 degree heat with the sun beating down on them? There are three things that make sports enjoyable that can also be applied to our work environment:

- *Rules.* All sports have rules that govern how to play the game. In business, we also need rules to live by.
- *Measurements.* How much fun would it be to play tennis and not know whether the ball landed on the other side of the court? You need to know how well you're doing, and it has to be personal. How popular do you think golf would be if the only feedback you got was that 200 people played golf last Saturday for an average score of ninety-three, and you had no way of knowing what your own score was?
- *Rewards.* Sports enthusiasts get their reward from trying to improve their game. Professionals see big dollars roll in and amateurs win trophies, but all of the rewards are tied into a measurement system. In business, we should all be pros or we shouldn't have a job. Sure, it's nice to get trophies, plaques, and dinners when we excel, but we should also receive financial rewards.

A measurement system is important for improvement for several reasons:
- It focuses attention on factors critical to achieving the organization's mission.
- It demonstrates effectiveness in resource use.
- It assists in setting goals and monitoring trends.
- It provides the input for analyzing root cause and the sources of errors.
- It identifies opportunities for ongoing improvement.
- It gives employees a sense of accomplishment.
- It provides a means of knowing whether you're winning or losing.
- It helps monitor progress.

Feedback is absolutely essential. Don't underestimate the importance of good quality data fed back rapidly to the individual performing the activity. Design your feedback and measurement system to provide:
- Meaningful data
- Timely feedback
- Accurate data
- Correct analysis
- An understandable format

Qualify the Process

Let's start this section with two definitions:

- *Certification* is a designed experiment applied to a single activity or piece of equipment. When the evaluating team is confident that the individual, activity, or piece of equipment, when following the related procedures, will provide output that meets the next activity requirement, the item is certified.

- *Qualification* is a designed experiment that involves evaluating a complex process consisting of many individual certified activities to determine whether the process can perform at an appropriate level when the activities are linked together. In addition, the process must demonstrate it can repeatedly deliver products and/or services on time, at the appropriate cost, and meet customer expectations on an ongoing basis.

The area most often overlooked is process qualification. We have a tendency to install a process and then put in a measurement system that identifies problems so that we can apply our problem-solving skills. We seem to like the thrill and excitement of having a lot of problems that must be solved right away. It's the way we get management's attention. A cynical saying at IBM was, "If you want to get promoted, generate a problem you know you can correct."

For example, if production control comes to the weekly project status meeting and reports that all the parts needed to support next week's production are in stock, their report gets no attention. But if the report shows that there are two part numbers out of 100,000 that aren't in stock and if they don't come in over the weekend, the production line will be down, suddenly everyone will be interested. They go on to report that they are flying two expediters back to the supplier on Friday to pick up the parts and bring them back to the plant on Saturday. They have scheduled receiving inspection to work on Sunday, and, if everything goes as planned, the parts will be on the line Monday morning at eight. The result is that management schedules a follow-up meeting Monday morning at seven to be sure the problem was solved. Then, when the production control manager reports to the group on Monday morning that everything went according to plan and the parts are on the line, the production control manager is the hero.

The real question should have been, why was it necessary to waste all that time and money because production control didn't do its job? To maintain process control, the process should be first qualified as being in control.

During the process qualification analysis, the process flow, equipment capabilities, process control points, training specifications, inputs, and cycle times are identified, analyzed, and validated. Processes used to create and deliver output to external customers should be qualified before the output is delivered to the first customer. This systematically helps the process to maximize its efficiency and effectiveness and ensure product performance. The same analysis can aid any organization in evaluating its business processes. Concepts such as capability, repeatability, and reliability should also apply to business processes. Because these processes mainly service internal customers, it's easy to lose sight of their importance to overall business survival. This is where process qualification helps by motivating us to take the first step toward continuous improvement. People love to be recognized for their efforts and are stimulated by public acknowledgments. Process qualification provides a system that instills a sense of pride and accomplishment within each team. Appendix C contains excerpts from a technical report, TR02.901, that describes how IBM qualifies its processes at its San Jose, California, location.

PHASE 3—REFINE THE PROCESS

In some cases, processes must be significantly improved before they can be qualified. It's a waste of effort to try to qualify a process that the organization knows isn't performing at an acceptable level. It's one thing to work on a process to continuously reduce variation and another to streamline a process, removing bureaucracy, waste, and duplication. Many processes should undergo major changes in the way they use information technology. In these cases, they must be refined and then requalified. Typical refinement projects that require qualification or requalification after they are implemented are:

- Systematic process breakthrough (business process improvement) methodologies
  - ☐ Process redesign
  - ☐ Process reengineering
  - ☐ Process benchmarking

- Information technology methodologies
  - ☐ Customer relationship management
  - ☐ SAP
  - ☐ B2B (business to business)
  - ☐ B2C (business to customer)
  - ☐ MRP II
  - ☐ Knowledge management

- New product processes
- Six Sigma projects

Once these types of projects are installed, the resulting processes should be qualified before they are considered complete.

Once a process is qualified, it's time to start refining it, continuously improving it from very good to excellent. However, it can't stop there. When you stop improving, you start slipping backward because your competition is also continuously improving. During phase 2, most PITs have collected a parking board (i.e., a list of items that need to be addressed at a later date) full of good ideas and improvement opportunities that are now ripe for harvesting. Most of the work that quality professionals do is related to continuously improving processes.

"Correction and focus on the process—not reacting to circumstances —results in increased leverage and improved organizational design and structure."
—William J. Schwarz

Refining a process is an ongoing activity. In most cases, the PIT focuses on the broad problems that reflect across departments and reaps this harvest within three to six months. At that time, the PIT can be disbanded and the process refinement activities turned over to the natural work teams (NWTs) that are involved in the process. The area activity analysis methodology discussed in chapter 3 relates easily to process refinement. If the refinement process is working as it should, the total process's efficiency and effectiveness should be improving at a rate of 10 to 15 percent a year.

Because the NWT's efforts are focused on subprocesses, there is some possibility of suboptimization occurring. For this reason, the process owner should continue to monitor the total process, using the established measurement system. If suboptimization or new cross-functional improvement opportunities occur, or if the process stops improving at an acceptable rate, the process owner should take action to address the situation.

By focusing on its processes and working with its suppliers, IBM reported that "Between 1997 and 2001, the hardware reliability of our high-end servers improved by more than 200 percent while computing power increased by a factor of four."

REPEAT PHASE 1—REDEFINE (DEFINE) THE PROCESS

"When everything is perfect,
remove something to force a new view."

—HJH

As an organization expends effort to refine a process, it reaches a point when additional refinement isn't practical. It's time to step back and take a fresh look at the process. To accomplish this, the reengineering methodology is most effective. With most processes, if technology hasn't restructured the process within the last five years, there is an opportunity for major improvement in the refined process. This leads the organization back to the beginning of phase 1. So the cycle is repeated time after time, always improving the process.

CHAPTER V

SYSTEMATIC PROCESS
BREAKTHROUGH METHODOLOGIES

"Select the right process. Then select the right improvement
methodology. Fail at either one, and your project will fail."

—HJH

Three methodologies make up the systematic process breakthrough approach, also
known as business process improvement. They are:

■ Process redesign
■ Process reengineering
■ Process benchmarking

The major processes selected to have systematic process breakthrough methodologies
applied to them (in order of the number of organizations that have selected the process)
are as follows:

■ Operations
■ Accounting and finance
■ Order management
■ Sales and marketing
■ Research and development/new product development
■ Supply chain management
■ Customer service
■ Information technology/management information services

"To compete in today's fast-changing environment, systematic
process breakthrough is a very important concept, although not
totally new."

—HJH

The question on everyone's mind is, "Considering my specific situation, which of the
systematic process breakthrough methodologies should I use to provide the most value to

my organization?" To answer this, you must first understand each of the three methodologies and select the appropriate one based upon your process's present condition and the amount of improvement it needs. The following discussion will help you make the correct selection.

PROCESS REDESIGN

The process redesign methodology takes an existing process and removes waste while reducing cycle time and improving the process's effectiveness. After the process is simplified, automation and information technology (IT) are applied, maximizing the process's ability to improve effectiveness, efficiency, and adaptability measurements. Process redesign is sometimes called focused improvement because it concentrates efforts on the present process. It results in improvements in effectiveness that range between 300 to 1,000 percent, and reduces cost and cycle times by 30 to 60 percent. Process redesign is the breakthrough methodology most frequently used because the risks are lower and the costs are less. This is the right answer for approximately 75 percent of business processes.

The process redesign approach to streamlining the business process consists of eleven tasks. They are:

Roller Skate Redesigned

- Bureaucracy elimination
- Value-added assessment
- Duplication elimination
- Simplification
- Cycle-time reduction
- Error-proofing
- Process upgrading
- Simplifying language
- Standardization
- Supplier partnership
- Automation, mechanization, computerization, and information technology

Figure 5.1 represents the typical effect a process redesign project has on cycle time. Note that it dropped the cycle time from thirty days to eighteen days in about six months. The

continuous improvement cycle continued to reduce cycle time by roughly 15 percent per year.

"Redesign requires 'out of the box' thinking to change the process to the point where it sets new benchmark standards."

—HJH

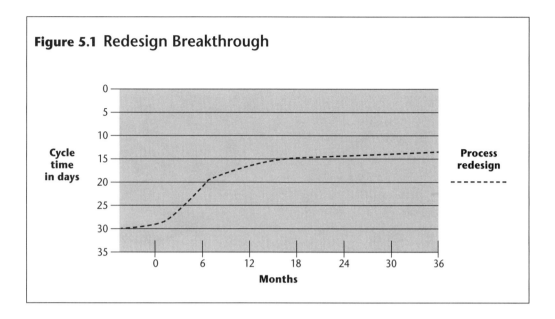

Figure 5.1 Redesign Breakthrough

The last task in the process redesign process is the use of IT enablers. To reduce the cost of implementing the IT solutions, they shouldn't be applied until the other ten tasks have been completed. In process redesign, best current IT practices are considered. E-business solutions during the 1990s were considered process reengineering applications because they pushed the envelope. Today they are considered current-state solutions and, as such, are process redesign tools. Advanced IT solutions include voice recognition, palm device applications, and radio frequency identification.

Peter Drucker points out that information-based organizations "can be built without advanced data processing technology."

Each time you consider removing or changing an activity, the simulation model should be updated to determine the effect on the total process. Frequently, an activity that is changed can positively affect a specific part of the process but negatively affect the total process. The simulation model allows you to quickly determine total effect. In many other cases, an activity can be changed in a number of different ways. Each of the options should be evaluated from a total process standpoint before one is selected. Continue to look for the best option, rather than settling for the first way of eliminating a root cause. Using process redesign, a process improvement team (PIT) can complete the new process design in about ninety days.

> "Reengineering is radical—revolutionary rather than evolutionary."
> —HJH

PROCESS REENGINEERING

• Roller Skate Reengineered •

Process reengineering is the most radical of the systematic process breakthrough methodologies. It's sometimes called process innovation because its success relies heavily on the PIT's innovative and creative abilities. Other organizations call this methodology "big picture analysis" or "new process design." The term "new process design" is the most appropriate because the approach used is the same as if the organization were designing the process for the first time. This approach takes a fresh look at the process objectives and ignores the present process and organizational structure. It's like starting with a blank sheet of paper, as you would if you were engineering the process for the first time.

Process reengineering, when applied correctly, reduces cost and cycle time between 60 to 90 percent and improves quality by 20 to 100 percent. It's a useful tool when the current process is so out of date it's not worth salvaging or even influencing the best-value future-state solution. Process reengineering is the correct solution for 5 to 15 percent of the major processes within an organization. If you find you're using process reengineering in more than 20 percent of your major processes, you should be concerned. It could indicate a major problem with the organization's management. This management problem should be addressed first, before a great deal of effort is devoted to improving processes that will not be maintained.

"'Reengineering' as a term carries negative connotations (e.g., terminations, downsizing, layoffs). We don't use it. Instead we focus on customer satisfaction and value-added processes."
—Controller of a $10 billion paper-goods firm

The process reengineering approach allows the PIT to develop a process that is as close to ideal as possible. The PIT steps back and takes a fresh look at the process, asking how the process would be designed if there were no restrictions. This approach takes advantage of available process enablers, including the latest mechanization, automation, and information technology techniques, and improves upon them. Often, this process stimulates the PIT to create a radical new process design that is a major breakthrough.

The process reengineering approach provides the biggest overall improvement, but it is also the most costly and time-consuming approach and has the greatest degree of risk associated with it. During the process reengineering cycle, the PIT will challenge all of the organization's sacred concepts as well paradigms related to the process being evalu-

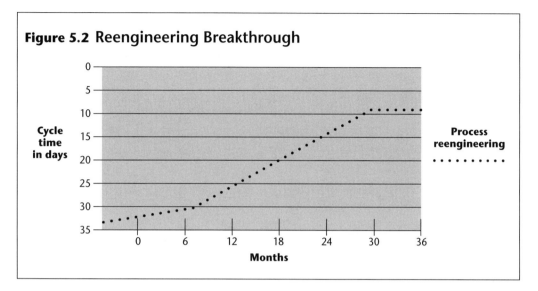

Figure 5.2 Reengineering Breakthrough

ated. The PIT is empowered to "make hamburger out of any sacred cow" that stands in the team's way of creating the ideal process. Often, the process reengineering approach includes organizational restructuring and can be very disruptive to the organization. Most organizations can only effectively implement one change of this magnitude at a time.

Figure 5.2 represents the typical effect a process reengineering project has on cycle time. Note that at the starting point, it took more than thirty days to go through the cycle. At the end of thirty-six months, the cycle time had been reduced to eight days.

The process reengineering approach to developing a best-value future-state solution consists of five tasks:

1. Big picture analysis
2. Theory of ones
3. Process simulation
4. Process modeling
5. Install the new process

Big Picture Analysis

Big picture analysis doesn't constrain the PIT in its vision. The results of process reengineering activities must be in line with the corporate mission and strategy. They should also reinforce the organization's core capabilities and competencies. Before the PIT starts to design the new process, it must understand where the organization is going, how the process being evaluated supports future business needs, and what changes would provide the organization with the most important competitive advantage.

Once this is understood, the PIT can develop a vision statement of what the best process would look like and how it would function. In developing the vision statement, the PIT needs to think outside the box and challenge all assumptions and constraints, question the obvious, identify the technologies and organizational structures that are limiting the process, and define how these factors can be used to create processes that are better than today's best. The vision statement defines only what must be done, not what is being done. Usually, the vision statement is between ten and thirty pages long and, in actuality, is more like a new process specification. The vision statement includes:

■ Definitions of what all stakeholders would like the process to look like
■ High-level process descriptions
■ A list of the potential people enablers
■ A list of the potential technology enablers
■ A list of the potential process enablers
■ A list of the potential organizational change enablers
■ A list of the potential organizational structure enablers
■ Projected performance specifications
■ Assumptions
■ A list of critical success factors

Theory of Ones

Once the vision statement has been finalized, the PIT should define what must be done within the process, from input to delivery to the customer. The team should question why the process can't be done in one activity by one person in one place or, better still, at one time with no human intervention. The PIT should be miserly about adding activities and resources to the process. To accomplish this, the team should use the "theory of ones" approach. (See figure 5.3.)

To use the theory of ones, the PIT sets the minimum quantity of units that the organization is trying to optimize. For example, if the PIT is interested in optimizing cycle time and the previous cycle time was five days, it might ask such questions as: "What if I had to do it in one second? What enablers would have to be used and what paradigms discarded to accomplish this?" Basically, four sets of enablers are addressed:

■ Process enablers
■ Personnel enablers
■ Information technology enablers
■ Organizational enablers

After the PIT has looked at each of the enablers to define how they could be used to create a new process that would accomplish the desired function, the resulting process is then compared to the vision statement. If the PIT gets an acceptable answer, it goes forward. If not, it repeats the cycle with the objective of doing the total process in one minute. At some point in time, the process and vision statement will harmonize. As you can see,

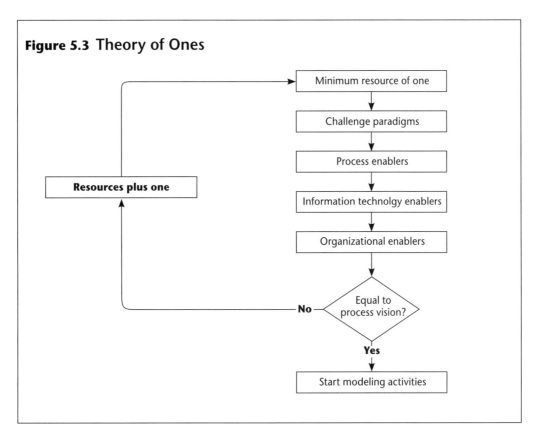

Figure 5.3 Theory of Ones

reengineering is an iterative process. Note that in the process redesign methodology, we look for ways to remove resources and waste. In the process reengineering methodology, we justify why it's necessary to add resources to the process.

Process Simulation

When the new process design (or future-state solution) is theoretically in line with the objectives set forth in the vision statement, a simulation model is constructed. The model is then evaluated to determine how the future-state solution will function. If the model proves to be unstable or produces unsatisfactory results compared to the requirements defined in the vision statement, the PIT reinitiates the theory of ones activity. Then the PIT prepares and evaluates a new simulation model. This cycle is repeated until an acceptable simulation model is constructed.

Process Modeling

Once the simulation model indicates that the future-state solution will meet the vision statement, the theoretical model is physically constructed to test the concepts. Typically the future-state solution will be evaluated as follows:

■ Conference room modeling (i.e., without computerization support) to verify the soundness of the new process design

■ Pilot modeling at an individual location or a small part of the organization to prove the details of the concepts individually

■ Pilot modeling of the entire process in a small part of the total organization

Install the New Process

With the successful completion of the pilot study, the future-state solution is ready for general rollout.

PROCESS BENCHMARKING

Benchmarking became a hot tool when Xerox credited it for helping the company drive its turnaround when it won the Malcolm Baldrige National Quality Award. Benchmarking is a popular tool that compares an organization's present process to the best similar processes available anywhere in the world. It might or might not compare processes from the same industry. Although benchmarking is not the approach normally selected, it provides a proven performance measurement that can be used to evaluate the excellence of the other two alternatives. It also provides the PIT with many good ideas that are often improved upon and included in the other two alternatives. Approximately 10 percent of the time benchmarking is the right solution.

In all organizations that have operations at more than one location, benchmarking activities should begin internally because of the ease of obtaining detailed data and cooperation. This step is often followed by external benchmarking activities. Often the external benchmarking process will focus on specific tasks or subprocesses that are defined as real value added or business value added during the streamlining process.

The ten business processes that are most often benchmarked are:

■ Information technology

■ Employee development and training

■ Document control and records management

■ Human resources

■ Customer service satisfaction

■ Performance measurement and improvement

■ Call centers and help desks

■ Accounting

■ Process improvement and management

■ Employee benefits compensation and incentive programs

(Source: The Benchmarking Exchange Six Sigma Survey, *www.benchnet.com*)

The benchmarking process consists of five phases. (See figure 5.4.) The five phases contain twenty activities. (See figure 5.5.)

Some of the benefits of benchmarking are:

- Defines the gap between the organization's performance and other organizations' performance, creating a desire to change
- Bases goals on external considerations and known performance standards
- Integrates best practices into the organization
- Creates goals that are more aggressive and credible
- Leads to faster implementation of new approaches with less risk
- Provides a better focus on external customers and consumers
- Develops effective measurement systems
- Improves individual and team creativity
- Provides many options to solve a single problem
- Results in breakthrough improvements
- Brings together the strategic plan and the organization's improvement efforts
- Breaks down old roadblock attitudes ("We've done that before.")
- Identifies strengths the organization can build on as well as weaknesses that must be improved

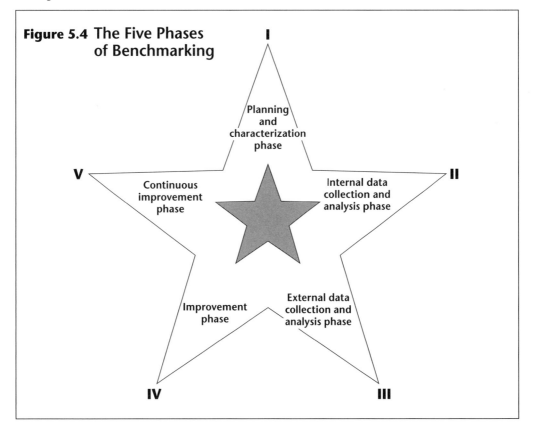

Figure 5.4 The Five Phases of Benchmarking

I — Planning and characterization phase

II — Internal data collection and analysis phase

III — External data collection and analysis phase

IV — Improvement phase

V — Continuous improvement phase

Figure 5.5 Twenty Activities of Benchmarking

Benchmarking Phase	Related Activities
Phase I Planning the benchmarking process and characterization of the item(s)	1. Identify what to benchmark. 2. Obtain top management support. 3. Develop the measurement plan. 4. Develop the data collection plan. 5. Review the plans with location experts. 6. Characterize the benchmark item.
Phase II Internal data collection and analysis	7. Collect and analyze internal published information. 8. Select potential internal benchmarking sites. 9. Collect internal original research information. 10. Conduct interviews and surveys. 11. Form an internal benchmarking committee. 12. Conduct internal site visits.
Phase III External data collection and analysis	13. Collect external published information. 14. Collect external original research information.
Phase IV Improvement of the item's performance	15. Identify corrective actions. 16. Develop an implementation plan. 17. Gain top management approval of the future-state solution. 18. Implement the future-state solution and measure its impact.
Phase V Continuous improvement	19. Maintain the benchmarking database. 20. Implement continuous performance improvement.

- Has a positive impact on employee pride and morale
- Is an important enabler that helps the organization compete for the Malcolm Baldrige National Quality Award
- Provides a high return on investment
- Helps the organization become the best it can be
- Develops valuable professional contacts
- Provides an excellent picture of the future-state solution before it is implemented
- Builds a high degree of cooperation among different functions and individuals within the organization

Figure 5.6 represents the typical effect that a process benchmarking project has on cycle time. Note that at this starting point, it took thirty days to go through the process. At the end of eighteen months, it has improved to only twenty days. The process then goes into its continuous improvement mode of operation.

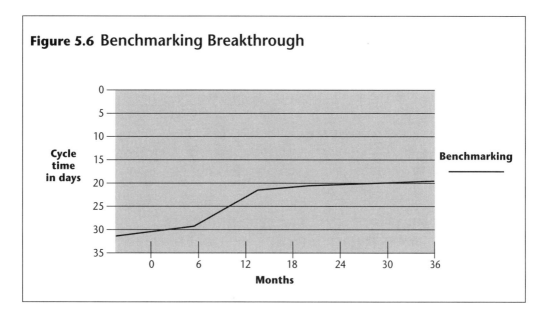

Figure 5.6 Benchmarking Breakthrough

Other Types of Benchmarking

There are three other types of benchmarking methodologies besides process benchmarking. They are:

- *Equipment benchmarking.* This applies to the technology that drives the organization. It's important to provide people with the best technology. Even the best employees are handicapped if they have to use obsolete and/or worn-out equipment. Targeted benchmarking equipment includes computers, software, telephone systems, information technology, manufacturing tools, office equipment, and robotics. The process involves comparing the level of performance of one potential supplier's products to another's.
- *Product benchmarking.* This is also sometimes called reverse engineering. It's the oldest type of commercial benchmarking. When an organization does product benchmarking, it purchases products from another organization and tests to see how the competitor's product is performing. These tests can take on many forms, including:
  - ☐ Life tests
  - ☐ Stress tests
  - ☐ Performance tests
  - ☐ Safety tests

Many consumer groups spend large amounts of money doing product benchmarking. A favorite target of consumer groups is the automobile industry. *Consumer Reports* is an excellent example of a consumer group that does product benchmarking.

However, although these consumer groups are good, they still don't provide the detailed information an organization should know about its competitor's products.

Commercial organizations go way beyond simply testing their competitors' products; they carefully disassemble them to see what makes them tick. This reveals a lot about the process that produced them, the components, the suppliers that were used, and the products' strengths and weaknesses.

■ *Service benchmarking.* This methodology sends a secret shopper into a shop, bank, store, hotel, airport, or other facility to buy products and/or services and keep detailed data about the service they received, the condition of the facilities, the type of people who waited on them, and many other factors. These observations are compared to the service offered by the secret shopper's organization to define improvement opportunities.

COMPARING THE THREE SYSTEMATIC PROCESS BREAKTHROUGH METHODOLOGIES

Let's compare the three systematic methodologies:

■ Process redesign
  □ Most frequently used because risks are lower, costs are less, and results happen faster
  □ Eighty to 100 days to develop the best-value future-state solution
  □ Cost and cycle time reductions of 30 to 60 percent
  □ Quality improvements of 40 to 100 percent
  □ Correct solution 75 percent of the time

■ Process reengineering
  □ Most radical of the three, with the greatest degree of risk
  □ Provides the biggest overall improvement but is the most costly, time-consuming, and risky option
  □ Nine to twelve months to develop the best-value future-state solution
  □ Cost and cycle time reductions of 60 to 90 percent
  □ Quality improvements of 20 to 100 percent
  □ Correct solution 15 percent of the time

■ Process benchmarking
  □ Ninety to 120 days to develop the best-value future-state solution
  □ Cost and cycle time reductions of 20 to 50 percent
  □ Quality improvements of 10 to 150 percent
  □ Correct solution 10 percent of the time

Figure 5.7 compares the three systematic process breakthrough methodologies.

Figure 5.7 Process Breakthrough Methodologies

	Redesign	**Reengineering**	**Benchmarking**
Reduce cost and cycle time	30 to 60 percent	60 to 90 percent	20 to 50 percent
Quality improvement	40 to 100 percent	20 to 100 percent	10 to 150 percent
Level of risk	Low	High	Medium
Percent of time with the correct answer	75 percent	15 percent	10 percent
Cycle time in months	2–3	9–12	3–4

Figure 5.8 shows the three improvement curves on a single graph. Although the process reengineering approach results in the best performance, process redesign came into play much faster and, for that reason alone, is often the best-value future-state solution for most situations.

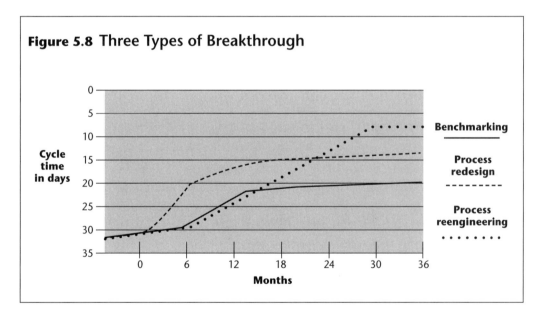

Figure 5.8 Three Types of Breakthrough

SET DIFFERENT CONSTRAINTS

Look at the same process in at least three different ways:

- What is the best process you can design if you have no constraints?
- What is the best process you can design if it had to be installed in *x* months?
- What is the best process you can design if you had only *y* dollars to spend?

By developing three different designs, you call upon different thinking patterns. (See figure 5.9.) Each of them generates a different set of solutions. Often the best total solution comes about when the three designs are combined, keeping the best ideas from each.

Figure 5.9 Process Constraints

	Original process	Constraints		
		No	**Cost**	**Time**
Performance				
Effectiveness	0.5	0.002	0.05	0.01
Efficiency	10.5 hours	4.2 hours	7.8 hours	6.5 hours
Adaptability	65 percent	88 percent	60 percent	73 percent
Cycle time	100 hours	40 hours	78 hours	65 hours
Cost per cycle	$1,000	$400	$750	$650
Implementation				
Cost		$1,500K	$500K	$800K
Cycle time		225 days	100 days	60 days
Probability of success		90 percent	90 percent	85 percent

FUTURE-STATE PROCESS DESIGN APPROVAL

After the future-state process design is completed, a detailed improvement cost and risk analysis must be made. This could include up to three alternative process designs. This analysis, along with the PIT's recommendations and a timeline implementation plan, should be presented to the executive team. It must then weigh the alternatives and decide how the organization's resources will be invested.

When the executive team approves future-state process designs, a project manager and a budget should be assigned to implement the new process design. The project manager will be responsible for pulling together the implementation team.

FINAL IMPLEMENTATION PLAN

The implementation team prepares a detailed implementation plan and coordinates the changes. The team might or might not include all members of the PIT. Often, depart-ment improvement teams become part of the implementation plan so that teams within the organization that will be effected by the changes are part of the group that plans and implements them. The implementation team can be divided into subteams (e.g., an information systems team).

The implementation plan is usually divided into three phases:

■ Short-term: changes that can be done in thirty days
■ Mid-term: changes that can be done in ninety days
■ Long-term: changes that require more than ninety days to implement

The final implementation plan for each change will include:

■ Schedule
■ Training requirements
■ Impact assessment
■ Modeling requirements
■ Data-collection process
■ Documentation plan

New Process Implementation Plan

The implementation plan and the change management plan are united at this point. The implementation team will maintain close control over each change to ensure correct implementation. Often, complex changes will go through a series of modeling and/or prototyping cycles to prove the concept and ensure smooth implementation.

After each change is installed, its effect is measured to ensure the change accomplishes its intent and has a positive effect on the entire process. Each time a change has been implemented, the simulation model is updated to reflect the present process.

In-Process Measurements

Before you can design a measurement system, you must define requirements. Each activity on the flowchart should be analyzed to establish customers' requirements as well as how the activity's efficiency will be evaluated.

A good measurement system is one in which the measurements are made as close to the activity as possible. Self-measurement is best because then there is no delay in corrective action. However, self-measurement is often impractical or impossible. Most business processes use a mixture of attributes and variables measurements. Of course, variables data are always preferable.

It's often necessary to measure and track each transaction as it moves through the process because, more often than not, it's not the average cycle time that loses customers but rather the exception that takes longer than usual or costs more than the customer expects. The improved process should not only improve averages but also reduce variation.

Feedback Systems

Without feedback to the person performing the task(s), measurement is just another no-value-added activity. Feedback always comes before improvement. In most organizations, too much data are collected and too little are used.

Employees need ongoing, positive and negative feedback about their output. Without this, it's like driving a car blindfolded. The feedback system should track averages and calculate control limits. The proper people should be notified whenever a point (i.e., transaction) falls outside of the negative control limit and the corrective action documented. Exception reporting is very important.

Poor Quality Cost

Waste costs money. In many business processes, poor quality cost runs as high as 80 percent of the budget. A poor quality cost of 50 percent or more is common in business processes.

Money is a common language for management and employees alike. You get everyone's attention when you translate poor performance into dollars. Saying, "I just blew a half-million-dollar sale" has a much greater effect than saying, "I just blew a sale."

> **"Our original development of the concept and quantification of quality cost has had the objective of equipping men and women throughout a company with the necessary practical tools and detailed economic know-how for identifying and managing their own cost of quality."**
> **—Armand V. Feigenbaum**
> **CEO, General Systems Co.**

A poor quality cost system provides management and employees with an excellent way of measuring progress. It can also be used to help define any rewards that may be given to the PIT for its efforts.

The third advantage of establishing a poor quality cost reporting system is that it prepares the organization for the continuous improvement activities that begin once the new process design is installed.

The three men who championed quality cost were Armand V. Feigenbaum, Philip B. Crosby, and myself.

During the early 1950s, Armand V. Feigenbaum, who was then vice president of GE, originated the concept of quality cost. It was made up of four categories:

- Prevention costs
- Appraisal costs
- Internal failure costs
- External failure costs

During the 1980s, Philip B. Crosby made cost of quality popular with his book, *Quality Is Free*. He used three categories:

- Prevention cost
- Appraisal cost
- Failure cost

Durning the 1960s, I was assigned to install a system to measure the cost of quality at IBM. I soon realized that, to get a true picture, Feigenbaum's four categories needed to be supplemented with some indirect quality costs. I also realized that the word "failure" was not well accepted in the support areas, so I changed it to "error." In the book, *Poor-Quality Cost* (ASQ Quality Press, 1987), I defined direct and indirect poor quality costs and their related categories.

I. Direct poor-quality costs

    A. Controllable poor-quality cost

        1. Prevention cost

        2. Appraisal cost

    B. Resultant poor-quality cost

        1. Internal error cost

        2. External error cost

    C. Equipment poor-quality cost

II. Indirect poor-quality costs

    A. Customer-incurred cost

    B. Customer-dissatisfaction cost

    C. Loss-of-reputation cost

> **"H. James Harrington in *Poor-Quality Cost* adds significant value to the development of the economics of quality and its utilization and management."**
> **—Armand V. Feigenbaum**
> **CEO, General Systems Corp.**

During the early 1990s another category—lost-opportunity cost—was added to the indirect poor quality costs. This is the revenue an organization doesn't realize due to poor judgment, missed market windows, or poor output that results in the organization being unable to take advantage of opportunities. Lost opportunities can exceed the total revenue. For example:

- Customers that switch to your competitor(s)
- Lost sales
- Products that come out too late (missed market windows)
- Effect of poor marketing estimates (average market estimate is 300 percent off).

> **"Reengineering (and redesign) are only effective when they are 100-percent supported by top management. Once recommendations have been made, top management must find ways to implement instead of reasons not to."**
> **—Controller, major nationwide retailer**

BIGGEST PROCESS IMPROVEMENT PROBLEMS

In a 2003 survey, *Quality Progress* magazine reported that the top process improvement problems were, in descending order:

- Lack of human resources to implement changes
- Results ignored by department heads
- Lack of financial resources to implement changes

- Problems communicating results
- Results ignored by senior executives

Keeping these five obstacles in mind, you should establish mitigation plans for each of them when you start a process improvement activity.

PROCESS IMPROVEMENT RECOGNITION AND REWARDS

An important part of keeping the process improvement activities going is to recognize both the individuals and teams responsible for the improvement ideas and those who expend effort to implement the ideas. An individual gets a lot of personal satisfaction from implementing a good idea, but the organization must reinforce this good behavior by recognizing it in some way. Stan Suring of Brady Corp. suggests, "Plan for incremental celebrations when a checkpoint has been reached. Don't be hesitant to acknowledge or downplay setbacks if and when they occur—they always do."

CHAPTER VI

TOTAL SIX SIGMA™

"Six Sigma has a problem-solving focus. You need Total
Six Sigma™ to excel by preventing problems."

—HJH

Probably the most popular performance improvement approach in use today is Six
Sigma, which was developed by Motorola during the mid-1980s and popularized in the
1990s when GE embraced it as its improvement approach.

HISTORY OF SIX SIGMA

In 1981, Motorola management realized that it had a major quality problem. The company had received a lot of bad press about how Matsushita Electric Industries of Japan had
improved the performance of Motorola's television holdings after the Japanese company
purchased it in 1974. At the time of sale, Motorola had three plants in the Chicago area
producing Quasar and Panasonic televisions. Matsushita achieved impressive results. For
example:

- Indirect personnel dropped almost 40 percent.
- Warranty costs dropped from $22 million a year to $3.2 million a year.
- The line reject rate dropped from 140 percent to less than 6 percent.
- Individual worker productivity improved by more than 30 percent.
- Rework and scrap decreased by 75 percent.
- Total plant output doubled.
- Both product lines were capturing a higher percentage of the U.S. market.

Many colleges throughout the United States were using Motorola as an example of poor
management. Based upon this experience and the organization's loss of market share in
its other product lines, in 1981 Motorola established a five-year, tenfold improvement in
quality as one of its top ten corporate goals. William J. Weisz, chief operating officer of
Motorola, explained, "This means that no matter what operation you are in, no matter
what your personal level of quality performance, whether you are in a service or manufac-

turing area, it is our goal to have you improve that level by an order of magnitude in the next five years." This goal led to a series of team and problem-solving training initiatives that were built around the total quality management (TQM) concept. These activities' objectives were to create a "quality culture" based upon people's values. This quality culture put the customer at the focal point of everything that Motorola did.

In a paper titled "The Birth of Six Sigma," Praveen Gupta wrote:

> "With any new technology initiative, awareness and understanding through education is the first step. Motorola University became the vehicle to transform Motorola into a high-performance organization. In this 'university,' managers were trained in change management to create a work culture that adapted to a challenging and competing environment. A strong management review process was also established. Some managers felt as though going to their management review meetings was like going to war because it was so thorough and tough. This management review was performed weekly, not monthly, as some experts suggest today."

(Complete text available online at *www.circuitsassembly.com.*)

During the first five years of this quality initiative, significant progress was made; however, economic conditions were still challenging. By 1986 Motorola realized that it needed a much more aggressive goal if it was going to regain its market share. As a result, in 1987 Motorola set a second cycle of tenfold improvement in four years as a corporate goal.

This presented Motorola with another challenge: how to measure a hundred times improvement in performance. If 10 percent of your cell phones are defective and you reduce that to zero, you have only accomplished 100-percent improvement. If you are running at five defects per unit and you reduce it to one defect per unit, you only get an 80-percent improvement.

Motorola's answer to this problem was to focus on the denominator rather than the numerator—in other words, three defects per 100 units reduced to three defects per 10,000 units, giving you a hundred times improvement.

Gupta points out:

> "Motorola's desire to be a leader in manufacturing in the core areas of communication, semiconductors, and industrial electronics led to a comprehensive benchmarking process for which best practices were searched. Phil Crosby's zero defects crusade was going on, with little success and challenges in implementation. Its biggest obstacle was opposition to achieving perfection because no one would commit to a perfect performance due to fear of failure."

This presented another problem: How do you determine the ratio when you may never produce a large enough population to measure it? Motorola embraced statistical applications to calculate the variance in the output based upon a small output sample size. As a result, the mathematics related to frequency distribution, developed by Walter A. Shewhart during the 1920s, became part of Motorola's quality improvement activities.

Gupta wrote:

> "During one feedback session from our quality management, I was told that, 'Motorola's corporate leaders were doing something more than three sigma.' I started looking into that concept and creating a measurement method beyond three sigma using normal distribution. Using four sigma limits, the defective parts per million becomes sixty-three parts per million. Knowing that the number of steps to manufacture semiconductor chips was about 200, four sigma appeared to be a satisfactory level of quality. With four sigma, cumulative yield was about 99 percent vs. about 67 percent using standard three sigma limits.

> "Bill Smith, a Motorola professional, had been contemplating a measurement method in a more realistic manner by allowing a shift of 1.5 sigma due to the assumption that processes behave normally and could fit Walter Shewhart's control chart theory. Accordingly, for a subgroup size of four, the control limits are set at 1.5 sigma. Therefore, for a normally controlled process, if the process average shifts by 1.5 sigma or more, the process must be shut down, which limits the maximum shift to 1.5 sigma. With these two issues in mind, Bill conceived and integrated the Six Sigma measurements and design for manufacturability methods. While developing these new methods, he had the total support of Bob Galvin, then-CEO of Motorola."

Figure 6.1 shows the difference in the number of possible errors at different sigma levels.

The next problem Motorola faced was normalizing a performance standard across many outputs of various complexities. This was overcome by using the total number of opportunities that could cause an error. For example, if there were 200 words on a page and the average number of letters in a word was eight, then there were 1,600 (200 x 8) opportunities to make an error on the page. Rather than talking about defects per million items (in this case, pages), they went to defects per million opportunities. Figure 6.2 shows examples of what sigma means. (Most organizations operate between three to four sigma.)

Motorola set an aggressive performance objective of six sigma for all outputs to internal and external customers. This represented an inherent process capability (Cp) of 2.0 or

Figure 6.1 Quality Levels and Corresponding Number of Errors

Quality level	Errors per 1,000 parts	Errors per million parts
1 sigma	317	317,310
2 sigma	45	45,500
3 sigma	2.7	2,700
3.5 sigma	0.465	465
4 sigma	0.063	63
4.5 sigma	0.0068	6.8
5 sigma	0.00057	0.57
6 sigma	0.000002	0.002

Figure 6.2 Examples of Sigma

Sigma level	Trip factor	Time lost by Big Ben	Revenue lost for damaged goods
+/- 3 sigma	Earth to Moon	9,071,000 seconds per century	$270,000 per $100 MM
+/- 4 sigma	Earth to Sun	216,000 seconds per century	$6,300 per $100 MM
+/- 5 sigma	Earth to end of solar system	1,800 seconds per century	$57 per $100 MM
+/- 6 sigma	Earth to end of galaxy	6 seconds per century	$.02 per $100 MM

0.002 errors per million opportunities. Motorola realized that over time the test population would vary plus or minus 1.5 sigma; therefore, it increased the error rate to 3.4 errors per million opportunities. This is an operational process capability (Cpk) of 1.5 that is better than the acceptable standard that was set in the early 1960s of a Cpk of 1.33.

To get the magnitude of improvement that was required, Motorola felt it needed to apply a much more sophisticated approach to problem analysis and corrective action than it was using. As a result, the company turned to design of experiments and Taguchi approaches that were being used in the TQM methodology. This required Motorola to train a number of employees in how to use these statistical methods. Moreover, the company determined that these employees needed various levels of expertise. Motorola classified these employees as:

- *Green Belt*—an individual trained to work in support of Six Sigma initiatives on a part-time basis. He or she generally works as a project team leader on problems and/or opportunities that are smaller in scale than the Black Belt projects.
- *Black Belt*—a full-time individual initially trained in quality management systems and advanced statistical tools and methods. He or she is assigned to work on critical business problems and/or opportunities, either alone or in teams.

- *Master Black Belt*—a full-time person who is responsible for teaching, mentoring, and reviewing Black Belts as well as for managing large-scale improvement projects

A great deal of time and effort can go into training Green and Black Belts. It takes four months to train a Black Belt; this includes one week per month of classroom training. A Black Belt class typically costs about $20,000 per student. When you consider that each Black Belt should save the organization at least $1 million per year, this doesn't seem like much to invest.

The American Society for Quality advertises a Yellow Belt class. It's a Web-based course designed to help Six Sigma teams familiarize themselves with the overall methodology and the basic process improvement tools. It teaches the student to be able to:

- Understand the benefits and implications of a Six Sigma program and relate the concepts to the overall business mission and objectives
- Communicate using Six Sigma concepts and language
- Recognize the organizational factors that are necessary groundwork for a successful Six Sigma program
- Use the sigma level concept to evaluate the capability of a process or organization
- Recognize the five-step define-measure-analyze-improve-control (DMAIC) model used to improve processes
- Apply basic process improvement tools within the DMAIC improvement model

Training for the Green, Black, and Master Black Belts is statistically oriented, as can be seen in Mikel J. Harry's series of books titled *The Vision of Six Sigma* (Tristar Publishing, 1997). The problem analysis cycle moved from the simple plan-do-check-act cycle developed by Walter A. Shewhart to a DMAIC cycle for process improvements and to a define-measure-analyze-design-verify (DMADV) cycle for new product/service development. (See Figure 6.3.)

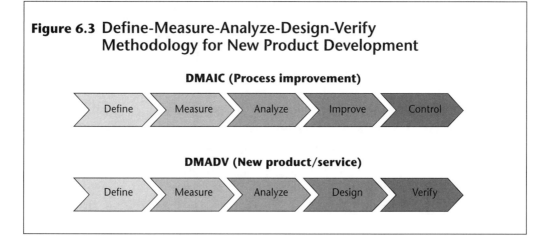

Figure 6.3 Define-Measure-Analyze-Design-Verify Methodology for New Product Development

DMAIC (Process improvement)

Define ▷ Measure ▷ Analyze ▷ Improve ▷ Control

DMADV (New product/service)

Define ▷ Measure ▷ Analyze ▷ Design ▷ Verify

Motorola provided a million hours of training per year to its employees. In 1987 it spent $44 million on training; this represented 2.4 percent of the corporation's payroll. Forty percent of the training was devoted to quality improvement processes, principles, techniques, and objectives. Motorola states that training programs on statistical process control, design for manufacturability, and understanding Six Sigma helped it to reach its ambitious goal of tenfold improvement in four years and started the organization on its continuous improvement route toward the Six Sigma objectives.

Six Sigma quality became popular immediately after Motorola won the Malcolm Baldrige National Quality Award in 1988. The information package that Motorola distributed to explain how it won stated:

> "To accomplish its quality and total customer satisfaction goal, Motorola concentrates on several key operational initiatives. At the top of the list is Six Sigma Quality, a statistical measure of variation from a desired result. In concrete terms, Six Sigma translates into a target of no more than 3.4 defects per million products, customer services included. At the manufacturing end, this requires designs that accommodate reasonable variation in component parts but production processes that yield consistently uniform final products. Motorola employees record the defects found in every function of the business, and statistical technologies are increasingly made part of each and every employee's job."

EXAMPLES OF SIX SIGMA IMPROVEMENT

Jack Welch, former CEO of GE, launched the Six Sigma program at that company with 200 projects in 1995. In 1996, the program increased to 3,000 projects. It expanded to 6,000 projects in 1997. The target for the Six Sigma program was to realize $150 million in productivity gains and profits. The actual 1997 savings was $320 million, more than double the goal. In 1998, net savings were estimated to be about $750 million.

Some people within GE were concerned because they believed Six Sigma would increase bureaucracy. Welch's reply to this concern was, "I don't give a damn if we get a little bureaucracy as long as we get the results."

Lawrence A. Bossidy, former GE vice chairman, started the Six Sigma program at Allied-Signal Inc. in 1991 when he was CEO. The results of increased productivity and profit got Jack Welch's attention. At the time GE was running at a three to four sigma level. The gap between four sigma and six sigma at GE was costing it between $8 to $12 billion a year.

William Woodburn, head of GE's industrial diamonds business, reports that in four years the operation's returns on investment increased fourfold, and the cost structure was cut in half. He gives the Six Sigma program credit for much of the improvement. To realize these improvements, he had to cut more than one-third of the workforce, which included more than 50 percent of the salaried staff. "Six Sigma has spread like wildfire across the company and is transforming everything we do," Welch observed. ("How Jack Welch Runs GE," *Business Week,* June 9, 1998.)

It's important to point out that Six Sigma is much more than Green, Black, and Master Black Belts. It's a total improvement process that follows TQM and the balanced scorecard. There are four major parts to Six Sigma as implemented by GE:

- Improvement process
  - ☐ Define products and services
  - ☐ Identify customer requirements
  - ☐ Compare products with requirements
  - ☐ Describe the process
  - ☐ Improve the process
  - ☐ Measure quality, productivity, and cycle time

- Quality measurements
  - ☐ Process mean and standard deviation
  - ☐ Process capability index
  - ☐ Defects per million units
  - ☐ Customer satisfaction

- Quality initiatives
  - ☐ Participative management
  - ☐ Short-cycle manufacturing
  - ☐ Design for manufacturability
  - ☐ Benchmarking
  - ☐ Statistical process control
  - ☐ Supplier qualification

- Improvement tools
  - ☐ Quality function deployment
  - ☐ Flowcharting
  - ☐ Pareto charts
  - ☐ Histograms
  - ☐ Cause-and-effect diagrams
  - ☐ Design of experiments
  - ☐ Process redesign

"We've generated an estimated $3.5 billion in savings through Six Sigma and digitization methodologies (during a six-year period)."
—Lawrence A. Bossidy
Chairman and CEO,
Honeywell International Inc.

GE's success with Six Sigma encouraged organizations around the world to start similar Six Sigma programs. Honeywell International is a good example. It trained all of its employees to the Green Belt level, 3,000 to the Black Belt level, and employs 100 Master Black Belts.

Dupont is another good example. It trained 10,000 employees to the Green Belt level. It has 1,200 Black Belts and 250 Master Black Belts.

What improvements has this generated? What is the return on investment? A survey conducted by Greenwich Associates found:

- Average cost for a project: $609,000
- Average return: $1,300,000
- Savings of $5 million or more are now routine.
- Gains for company with three years' experience are 13 percent higher.
- The measure stage of DMAIC is the most difficult.

It's important to note that this same effect can occur as operators are changed on the same equipment or between different sets of equipment used in the same process to do the same activity. Equipment presents an additional problem because both the mean and the distribution can be different between equipment and fixtures built to the same specification. Figure 6.4 shows how quality levels vary based on off-center drifts expressed in sigmas.

You can see that there are a number of ways to achieve a quality level of 3.4 defects per million parts or fewer. Here are four typical examples:

Figure 6.4 Variations in Quality Levels

Number of defectives (parts per million) for specified off-centering of the process and quality levels

Off-centering quality level	3 sigma	3.5 sigma	4 sigma	4.5 sigma	5 sigma	5.5 sigma	6 sigma
0	2,700	465	63	3.4	0.57	0.034	0.002
0.25 sigma	3,577	666	99	12.8	1.02	0.1056	0.0063
0.5 sigma	6,440	1,382	236	32	3.4	0.71	0.019
0.75 sigma	12,288	3,011	665	88.5	11	1.02	0.1
1 sigma	22,832	6,433	1,350	233	32	3.4	0.39
1.25 sigma	40,111	12,201	3,000	577	88.5	10.7	1
1.50 sigma	66,803	22,800	6,200	1,350	233	32	3.4
1.75 sigma	105,601	40,100	12,200	3,000	577	88.4	11
2 sigma	158,700	66,800	22,800	6,200	1,300	233	32

- With 0 sigma off-centering with 4.5 sigma quality
- With 0.5 sigma off-centering with 5 sigma quality
- With 1 sigma off-centering with 5.5 sigma quality
- With 1.5 sigma off-centering with 6 sigma quality

It's much easier to center the mean than it is to reduce variation significantly. Pandu R. Tadikamalla, a professor at the University of Pittsburgh, points out:

> "Over 1,200 such projects are underway, and in 2003 we will more than double that number. Many of the 4,000 completed projects have resulted in reduced environmental impact or increased safety."
> —**Chad Holliday**
> **CEO, Dupont**

> "When companies embark on Six Sigma quality programs, what is their objective? Is it to reduce the process variance so that the half-tolerance of the product characteristic is equal to six times the standard deviation? Or is it to have very few defects, say in the neighborhood of 50 to 100 per million? From the technical viewpoint, it might make sense to talk in terms of the process variance. From the managerial or customer viewpoint, the quality standards can be described in terms of defects per million. In addition, in many situations, adjusting the process to move the process average closer to the target value is relatively easier than improving the process to reduce the variance. Thus, if the goal is to reduce the number of defects, it does not make much sense to improve the process to Six Sigma levels and not center the process. Planning or allowing for the process average to drift 1.5 standard deviations from the target value just in case is similar to building up inventories when implementing just-in-time inventory management."[1]

A debate on Six Sigma or allowable off-center drift isn't time well spent. The important thing is the output quality level, expressed in parts per million or parts per billion. Figure 6.5 is a chart prepared by Fred McFadden, a professor at the University of Colorado. It was published in "Six Sigma Quality Programs" in the June 1993 issue of *Quality Progress*. It provides an excellent example of defect rate decrease as the sigma specification level ratio increases.

Although 3.4 errors per million fuses, bolts, screws, nuts, garden hoses, or brooms might not be an aggressive target, when you start to apply the same requirements to management decisions, drawings, books, letters, sales contracts, meals served, auto repairs, medical operations, sales calls, or lines of codes, it becomes a very aggressive target indeed. This is particularly true in any type of service activity where quality can't be inspected or tested. Motorola chairman of the board and CEO George Fisher stated: "Improvements in product quality seem to be stalled at the 5–5.2 sigma wall."

1 Tadikamalla, Pandu R. "The Confusion Over Six Sigma Quality." Quality Progress, Vol. 27, No. 11. 1994.

Figure 6.5 Defect Rate Decrease and Sigma Specification Increase

Defect rate vs. sigma level (centered process) sigma level

Sigma level	Error rate (ppm)	Duration of power outages per month	Number of misspelled words
1	317,400	228.5 hours	159 per page
2	45,600	32.8 hours	23 per page
3	2,700	1.94 hours	1.35 per page
4	63	2.72 minutes	1 per 31 pages
5	0.57	1.48 seconds	1 per several books
6	0.002	0.005 seconds	1 per small library
7	0.000003	0.00001 seconds	1 per large library

The Six Sigma program isn't just a new performance standard. Its parameters cannot be met if an organization does the same old thing the same old way. It is for this reason that Motorola calls it the Six Sigma Quality Program because it drove a major improvement effort that radiated through the organization.

DO YOU NEED SIX SIGMA PROCESSES?

Many managers question if their organizations need to operate at 3.4 errors per million opportunities. Perhaps not if you have only one part and one activity. But if you are putting together 50 parts that are at three sigma, 3.15 percent of the assemblies will be defect-free. Or if you process a document through ten operations with only one measurement that was at 3 sigma at each operation, more than 50 percent of the documents would have errors in them.

In other words, you have a near-zero possibility of getting an acceptable product through the process without repair. This is assuming that all the parts or steps are in series with each other. Figure 6.6 provides a breakdown of this concept based upon the number of steps or parts in the process, and various sigma limits, assuming a 1.5 sigma shift. (Source: Six Sigma Research Center.)

Many other organizations have embraced Six Sigma concepts. Among them are IBM, Texas Instruments, and Defense System Electronics Group. Most quality-focused organizations performed at the 4 sigma level at the beginning of the 1990s. As of this date, I know of no organization that is performing all of its measurements to the Six Sigma requirements. Six Sigma and the related methodologies are not implemented without difficulties.

Figure 6.6 Throughput Yield vs. Process Steps and Quality

Throughput yield vs. number of process steps and process quality

Number of parts and/or process steps	Process sigma level (assume 1.5 sigma shift)			
	3 sigma	4 sigma	5 sigma	6 sigma
1	93.32%	99.379%	99.9767%	99.99966%
2	87.09	98.76	99.95	99.99932
5	70.77	96.93	99.88	99.9983
10	50.09	93.96	99.77	99.9966
50	3.15	73.24	98.84	99.98
100	0.10	53.64	97.70	99.966
500	0	4.44	89.02	99.83
1,000	0	1.2	79.24	99.66
2,000	0	0	62.75	99.32

GE has embraced Six Sigma to drive its future quality improvement activities. GE's Six Sigma program is the largest quality initiative ever mounted in the United States. GE calls its approach Design for Six Sigma, DMADV, which stands for:

- *Define.* Define the process, product, or service that will be improved. Define the customer's view of error-free performance.
- *Measure.* Evaluate the current item's performance.
- *Analyze.* Define best practices, benchmarks, and enablers.
- *Design.* Develop a best-value future-state solution.
- *Verify.* Measure the new item to ensure it meets the requirements documented in the define stage and in the Six Sigma requirements.

The Six Sigma approach to quality improvement is being adopted throughout all of GE's divisions. Jack Welch stated that the Six Sigma program added $5 billion to GE's net earnings through the year 2000.

The following tools and techniques are used by GE in support of Six Sigma. (This is not a complete list, but it does provide a representative sample.)

- Quality function deployment
- Visioning
- Benchmarking
- Statistical process control
- Root cause analysis
- Critical source factors
- Charters

- Stratification
- Regression analysis
- Design of experiments
- Cause-and-effect analysis
- Force field analysis
- Brainstorming
- Process mapping
- Shareholder analysis
- Prioritization matrix
- Problem cycle
- Surveys
- Focus groups
- Process frame (boxing)
- Organizational change management
- Gantt chart
- Project management
- Common/special causes
- Pareto charts
- Process capability
- Scatter diagrams
- Histogram
- The 5 Ws
- Value-added analysis
- Cycle time/workflow analysis
- Charting (pie, bar, etc.)
- Affinity diagrams
- Process analysis
- Activity-based costing
- Work-out
- Gap analysis
- Moments of truth
- Value analysis
- Quantifying opportunities
- Resistance analysis
- Cost-benefit analysis
- "Should be" process maps
- Behavior conditioning
- Classification of solution criteria
- Mind mapping

- Risk assessment
- Work breakdown structure
- Continuous improvement
- Standardization
- Measurement plan

EVOLUTION OF TOTAL SIX SIGMA™

Since its conception by Motorola in 1987, the scope and content of the Six Sigma methodology has continued to expand and has now evolved into a total improvement process. Six Sigma has changed and expanded so radically that it's very different today than it was when Motorola started it. Today, organizations should be using Total Six Sigma™.

Total Six Sigma™ represents the expansion of the Six Sigma concepts to cover all of the key attributes of TQM and lean, plus the effective use of information technology as an essential enabler to improve organizational performance. It also integrates into the Six Sigma methodology a sophisticated organizational change management methodology designed to prepare the organization for the cultural shifts necessary to function at the six sigma level and give the organization the resiliency it needs to continuously refine and improve its operations.

Total Six Sigma™ includes all of the tools and methodologies in the present Six Sigma approach and adds additional methodologies necessary to maximize the total return on investment. Other tools included in Total Six Sigma™ are:

- Management transformation
- Strategic planning
- Team building
- Organizational change management
- Statistical process control
- Area activity analysis
- Balanced scorecard
- Reward-and-recognition systems
- Information technology enablers
- Knowledge management systems
- Supplier improvement initiatives
- Creativity enhancement
- Certification classes for Green, Black, and Master Black Belts, and Champions
- Distance learning courses on performance improvement
- Process simulation
- Process reengineering and redesign

- Measuring executive error rates
- Three-year improvement plans
- Supply-chain management
- Lean Six Sigma
- Risk management
- Quick and easy *kaizen*

A total approach to improving organizational performance is required in most organizations, one that takes advantage of the improvement training and programs the organization already uses or has used. It's imperative that employees don't feel that the effort they expended in the past is wasted. Total Six Sigma™ builds upon the organization's strength while correcting any weakness that is preventing the organization from meeting its goals. Everyone must focus on performance improvement. Some organizations have increased the number of suggestions submitted per employee from an average of 0.8 per year to twenty-four per year. The Green Belts, Black Belts, and Master Black Belts play an important role in solving the critical problems (few in number), but major progress can also be made by harnessing the power of the entire workforce and focusing its efforts on the many small problems that occur daily. Remember: There's never a problem so small that you can't lose a customer because of it.

Experience proves that good project management and change management methodologies are an important part of implementing a successful Six Sigma process. The primary difference from GE's Six Sigma process and the ones that failed aren't the tools that were used but the way the program was implemented. Six Sigma goals for major processes usually aren't met unless the processes are redesigned or reengineered using a sound, proven methodology.

The last point that must be discussed is the effective use of all of the enablers available to you. These include:

- People enablers
- Process enablers
- Information technology enablers
- Knowledge enablers
- Change enablers

In most organizations that have installed a Six Sigma process, the information technology, knowledge, and change enablers haven't been used or at least haven't been used effectively. Without the effective use of tools such as portals, a knowledge warehouse, knowledge maps, customer relationship management software, portfolio project management software, balanced scorecards, corrective action tracking systems, and change mapping, the full benefit of a Six Sigma program can't be obtained.

Some organizations achieve performance improvement with a 40:1 return on investment while others have lost money in their quest for excellence. You need experienced change experts and process experts to minimize your risks and maximize your return on investment.

IMPLEMENTING TOTAL SIX SIGMA™

There are four phases, which include thirty-three different tasks, involved in implementing a Total Six Sigma™ project in an organization:

- Phase 1—Assessment
  1. Assess current status and opportunities.
  2. Benchmark Six Sigma organizations.
  3. Define gaps.
  4. Create the business case.
  5. Make the Total Six Sigma™ decision.
  6. Assign an executive management Total Six Sigma™ support team.

- Phase 2—Planning
  1. Define business drivers.
  2. Prepare vision statements for each business driver.
  3. Prepare a balanced scorecard.
  4. Prioritize the business processes.
  5. Define improvement approaches.
  6. Identify internal resources for potential Black Belt and Champion assignments.
  7. Define overall measurements system.
  8. Identify pilot area.
  9. Develop the Total Six Sigma™ awareness plan.
  10. Create a Total Six Sigma™ project plan:
      ☐ Mission
      ☐ Goals
      ☐ Change management plan
      ☐ Schedule
      ☐ Tools
      ☐ Training
      ☐ Budget

  11. Approve overall budget.

- Phase 3—Implementation
    1. Develop training materials.
    2. Executive training (one day).
    3. Select and train champions (one week).
    4. Total Six Sigma™ general population awareness and tools training
    5. Select and train Black Belts for first cycle.
    6. Develop the rewards and recognition system.
    7. Assign Black Belts to first cycle projects.
    8. Review results of first cycle.
    9. Train Green Belts and assign them to the second cycle.
    10. Install other parts of the Total Six Sigma™ methodology as defined in the project plan.
    11. Measure effect.
    12. Conduct executive management Total Six Sigma™ support team project reviews.

- Phase 4—Continuous improvement
    1. Implement area activity analysis.
    2. Recycle Black Belts and assign new projects.
    3. Update yearly objectives.
    4. Reward significant contributors to the success of the Total Six Sigma™ initiative.

A 2003 *Quality Digest* Six Sigma survey reported that the average cost per employee to implement a Six Sigma process is $100 to $200 per employee. This cost varied from $600 to $31.42. Costs decreased for bigger organizations. (See figure 6.7.) The survey also revealed that most organizations thought that Six Sigma and TQM utilized the same tools. The following are some key results from respondents of this survey:

- Overall cost of quality system failure was less than 0.5 percent of sales. We were benchmarked as the top quality supplier for 90 percent of our customers.
- $2.3 million in savings since 2002
- During a nine-month period: 21 completed projects, $1 million in savings, increased accurate forecasting and production planning by 60 percent

Figure 6.7 Six Sigma Improvement Survey

	Agree	Disagree	Neutral
Improved organization's profitability	72%	14%	14%
Improved job satisfaction	53%	23%	24%
Improved customer satisfaction	54%	27%	19%

- $2 billion in savings
- $25,000 per month savings
- $55 million in hard savings, $120 million in soft savings
- Greater than $1.5 billion in benefits
- Reduced waste: $150 million
- $5 million in savings corporatewide
- Customer complaints reduced by 75 percent. Productivity increased by 5 percent
- Approximately $8 million per year for our location
- Reduced manufacturing cycle time by 75 percent, decreased resource costs to process received goods by 57 percent, reduced eco-process cycle time by 97 percent, reduced manufacturing errors by 82 percent

CHAPTER VII

PROCESS MATURITY GRID

"Too few organizations understand how good their processes can be because they have no measure of how bad they are."

—HJH

Qualification usually is a one-time event because it's designed to validate that a process can perform to its designed specification. But today, organizations that want to excel have expanded this concept to evaluate their businesses' maturity. For example, the software industry has agreed to a five-level process development maturity grid. A six-level maturity grid should be used for all business processes. (See figure 7.1.)

To determine whether a process has evolved to the next level, eight major change areas are addressed:

- End-customer-related measurements
- Process measurements and/or performance
- Supplier performance
- Documentation
- Training
- Benchmarking
- Process adaptability
- Continuous improvement

Figure 7.1 Six-Level Process Maturity Grid

Level	Status	Description
6	Unknown	Process status hasn't been determined.
5	Understood	Process design is understood and operates according to prescribed documentation.
4	Effective	Process is systematically measured, streamlining has started, and end-customer expectations are met.
3	Efficient	Process is streamlined and more efficient.
2	Error-free	Process is highly effective (i.e., error-free) and efficient.
1	World-class	Process is world-class and continues to improve.

For each level, a set of requirements has been established. The requirements are more stringent as you move up in the levels. Figure 7.2 shows the six levels vs. the eight items. As the shade gets darker, the requirements become closer to world-class status.

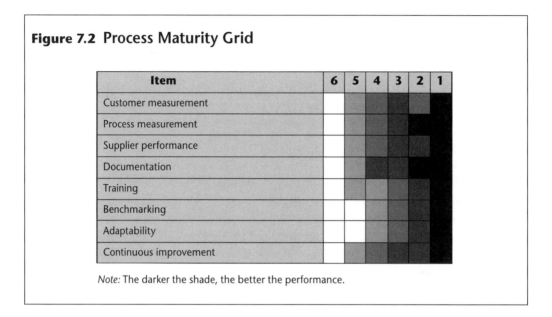

Figure 7.2 Process Maturity Grid

Item	6	5	4	3	2	1
Customer measurement						
Process measurement						
Supplier performance						
Documentation						
Training						
Benchmarking						
Adaptability						
Continuous improvement						

Note: The darker the shade, the better the performance.

REQUIREMENTS FOR LEVEL FIVE QUALIFICATION

Qualification at level five signifies that the process design is understood by the process improvement team (PIT) and is operating to the prescribed documentation.

All processes are classified as level six until sufficient data have been collected to determine their true status. Normally, processes move from a qualification level six to a qualification level five. To be qualified at any level, all the criteria in each of the eight major change areas (e.g., supplier performance, process measurements, and/or performance) must be met or exceeded. The criteria for level five are:

■ End-customer-related measurements
  ☐ Measurements reflect the end-customer's view of the process.
  ☐ End-customer requirements are documented.
  ☐ An end-customer feedback system is established.
  ☐ End-customer effectiveness charts are posted and updated.

■ Process measurements and/or performance
  ☐ Overall effectiveness and efficiency are measured and posted where they can be seen by employees.

☐ Effectiveness and efficiency targets are set.

☐ Process operational and/or control weaknesses are evaluated and meet minimum requirements.

■ Supplier performance
☐ All suppliers are identified.

■ Documentation
☐ Process is defined and flowcharted.
☐ Flowchart accuracy is verified.
☐ Documentation is followed.
☐ PIT members and process owners are named.
☐ PIT mission is documented.
☐ Process boundaries are defined.

■ Training
☐ PITs are trained in the basic tools and the fundamental business process improvement tools.
☐ In-process training needs are evaluated and documented.
☐ Resources are assigned to support training needs.

■ Benchmarking
☐ Not required

■ Process adaptability
☐ Not required

■ Continuous improvement
☐ Basics of business process improvement are in place.
☐ All major exposures are identified, and action plans are in place.
☐ A detailed plan to improve the process to level four is agreed upon and funded.

REQUIREMENTS FOR LEVEL FOUR QUALIFICATION

When a process evolves to qualification level four, it is called an effective process. Processes qualified at level four have a systematic measurement system in place that ensures end-customer expectations are met. The process has started to be streamlined.

To be qualified at level four, the process must be able to meet all the requirements for level five, plus the following requirements:

■ End-customer-related measurements
  ☐ End-customer requirements are met.
  ☐ End-customer expectations are documented.

■ Process measurements and/or performance
  ☐ Overall effectiveness targets are met, and challenge targets are established by the PIT.
  ☐ Poor quality cost measurements are developed.
  ☐ Some internal efficiency measurements are established.
  ☐ Internal effectiveness measurements and targets are 50-percent complete and posted.
  ☐ Overall process cycle time and cost are defined.
  ☐ No significant effectiveness, efficiency, or control exposures exist.
  ☐ Substantial improvement activities are underway.

■ Supplier performance
  ☐ Meetings are held with critical suppliers, and agreed upon input requirements are documented.
  ☐ All critical suppliers meet input requirements.

■ Documentation
  ☐ Process is flowcharted, and documents are updated.
  ☐ Overall process is fully documented.
  ☐ Documentation of subprocesses has started.
  ☐ Readability is evaluated.

■ Training
  ☐ In-process job training procedures are developed for all critical activities.
  ☐ People are assigned to conduct job and process training.
  ☐ PIT is trained in statistical process control.

■ Benchmarking
  ☐ Plan exists to benchmark end-customer requirements.

■ Process adaptability
  ☐ Data are collected that identify problems with present process adaptability.

■ Continuous improvement
  ☐ Process is operational, and control weaknesses are assessed and deemed containable.

☐ A plan for improving the process to level three is prepared, approved, and funded.

☐ The process philosophy accepts that people make mistakes, provided everyone works relentlessly to find and remove causes of errors.

REQUIREMENTS FOR LEVEL THREE QUALIFICATION

When a process evolves to qualification level three, it is called an efficient process. Processes qualified at level three have completed the streamlining activities, and there has been a significant improvement in the efficiency of the process.

To be qualified at level three, the process must be able to meet all the requirements for levels five and four, plus the following:

- End-customer-related measurements
    ☐ End-customer expectations are met.
    ☐ Challenge targets are set by the PIT.

- Process measurements and/or performance
    ☐ There is a significant improvement in process quality.
    ☐ Internal effectiveness and efficiency measurements are in place and are posted. Targets are set for the affected areas.
    ☐ There is a significant reduction in cycle time and bureaucracy.
    ☐ Overall efficiency targets are met.
    ☐ Most measurements show an improvement trend.
    ☐ Key process control points are identified.
    ☐ Tangible, measurable results are realized.

- Supplier performance
    ☐ Meetings are held with all suppliers, and agreed-upon input requirements are documented.
    ☐ All critical suppliers meet input requirements.

- Documentation
    ☐ Subprocesses are documented.
    ☐ Training requirements are documented.
    ☐ Software controls are in place.
    ☐ The readability level of all documents is at a grade level less than the minimum education of the people using them.
    ☐ Employees understand their job descriptions.

- Training
  - ☐ All people performing critical jobs are trained in the new procedures, including job-related training.
  - ☐ In-process job-training procedures are developed for all activities.
  - ☐ Plans are in place to train all employees who are part of the process in team methods and problem-solving tools.
  - ☐ PIT understands one or more of the ten sophisticated tools of business process improvement.
  - ☐ All employees in the process receive training on the entire process operation.

- Benchmarking
  - ☐ End-customer requirements are benchmarked.
  - ☐ A plan exists to benchmark critical activities.
  - ☐ A plan exists to benchmark the process.

- Process adaptability
  - ☐ Employees are trained to distinguish how far they can deviate from the established procedures to meet a customer's special needs.
  - ☐ Future process change requirements are projected.
  - ☐ A proactive internal and external customer complaint system is established.
  - ☐ The end-customer has reviewed the process change plan and agreed that it meets his or her needs during the strategic period.

- Continuous improvement
  - ☐ A plan to improve the process to level two is developed, approved, and funded.

REQUIREMENTS FOR LEVEL TWO QUALIFICATION

When a process has evolved to qualification level two, it is called an error-free process. Processes qualified at level two are highly effective and efficient. Both external and internal customer expectations are measured and met. Rarely is there a problem within the process. Schedules are always met, and stress levels are low.

To be qualified at level two, the process must be able to meet all the requirements for the previous qualification levels, plus the following requirements:

- End-customer-related measurements
  - ☐ End-customer expectations are updated.
  - ☐ Performance for the past six months never fell below end-customer expectations.
  - ☐ The trend lines show continuous improvement.

☐ World-class targets are established.

☐ End-customers are invited to regular performance reviews.

☐ End-customer desires are understood.

■ Process measurements and/or performance

☐ All measurements show an improvement.

☐ Benchmark targets are defined for external customers and critical in-process activities.

☐ In-process control charts are implemented as appropriate, and the process is under statistical control.

☐ Feedback systems are in place close to the point where the work is being done.

☐ Most measurements are made by the person doing the job.

☐ There is tangible and measurable improvement in the in-process measurements.

☐ No operational inefficiencies are anticipated.

☐ An independent audit plan is in place and working.

☐ The process is error-free.

■ Supplier performance

☐ All supplier inputs meet requirements for the past three months.

☐ Regular meetings are held to ensure that suppliers understand the changing needs of and expectations about the process.

■ Documentation

☐ Change level controls are in place.

☐ Documents are systematically updated.

■ Training

☐ All employees in the process are trained and scheduled for refresher courses.

☐ Employee evaluation of their training process is complete, and the training meets all employee requirements.

☐ Team and problem-solving courses are complete. Employees are meeting regularly to solve problems.

■ Benchmarking

☐ Process is benchmarked, and targets are assigned.

☐ PIT understands the keys to the benchmark organization's performance.

■ Process adaptability

☐ Employees are empowered to provide the required emergency help to their customers and are measured accordingly.

☐ Resources are committed to satisfy future customer needs.

☐ Process adaptability complaints are significantly reduced.

■ Continuous improvement

☐ The process philosophy has evolved to the point at which errors are unacceptable.

☐ Everyone works relentlessly to prevent errors from occurring, even once.

☐ Surveys of the employees show that the process is easier to use.

☐ Plans to improve the process to level one are prepared, approved, and funded.

☐ The process measurement trend line indicates that the process has improved at an annual rate of at least 10 percent in 75 percent of the measurements, and there are no negative trends.

REQUIREMENTS FOR LEVEL ONE QUALIFICATION

Qualification level one is the highest qualification level. It indicates that the process is one of the ten best processes of its kind in the world, or it is in the top 10 percent of like processes, whichever has the smallest population.

Processes that reach qualification level one are world-class. Processes qualified at level one have proven that they are among the best in the world. These processes are often benchmark target processes for other organizations. As a rule, few processes in an organization ever get this good. Processes that reach level one are truly world-class and continue to improve to maintain their status.

To be qualified at level one, the process must be able to meet all the requirements for the previous qualification levels, plus the following:

■ End-customer-related measurements

☐ End-customer expectation targets are regularly updated and always exceeded.

☐ World-class measurements are met for a minimum of three consecutive months.

☐ Many of the end-customer desires are met.

■ Process measurements and/or performance

☐ All measurements exceed those of the benchmark organization for the past three months.

☐ Effectiveness measurements indicate that the process is error-free for all end-customers and in-process control points.

■ Supplier performance

☐ All suppliers meet process expectations.

☐ All suppliers met process requirements for a minimum of six months.

■ Documentation
  ☐ All documents meet world-class standards for the process being improved.

■ Training
  ☐ Employees are regularly surveyed to define additional training needs, and new training programs are implemented based on these surveys.

■ Benchmarking
  ☐ An ongoing benchmarking plan is implemented.

■ Process adaptability
  ☐ During the past six months, no customers complained that the process did not meet their needs.
  ☐ The present process handles exceptions better than the benchmark organization's process.

■ Continuous improvement
  ☐ All process measurement trend lines indicate that the process is improving at an annual rate of at least 15 percent.
  ☐ An independent audit has verified world-class status.
  ☐ Plans are approved and in place to become even better.

It's important to note that the goal for all level-one processes is to go beyond world-class to become a "best of breed" process. Although some processes become best-of-breed for short periods of time, it's difficult to stay No. 1. It requires a great deal of work and creativity, but the personal satisfaction is well worth it.

For more information related to process maturity grids, see my book, *Business Process Improvement* (McGraw-Hill, 1991).

CHAPTER VIII

PROCESS MANAGEMENT EXCELLENCE SUMMARY

"Our processes are never so good that they can't improve. New eyes, new ears, and an open mind are all it takes."

—HJH

There are hundreds of examples of how applying process improvement methodologies have saved organizations money, reduced cycle time, and improved quality. The following are five excellent examples of process improvements reported in the Spring 2003 issue of the *Journal of Quality and Participation*.

■ Fidelity Wide Processing—Incoming Customer Correspondence Process Improvement Team:

"The purpose of the team was to improve service delivery to customers, increase production efficiencies, and reduce unit cost. Using quality tools and teamwork, service delivery increased by 31 percent, productivity improved by 33 percent, unit costs were reduced by 32 percent, quality improved by 52 percent, and $1.9 million was saved annually."

■ Grain Processing Corp.—Weight Watchers:

"This team was tasked with eliminating overweight and underweight railcars, maximizing freight, and reducing costs. Several problem-solving methods were used to identify root causes and identify a solution. Results included improving customer satisfaction with more on-time deliveries, boosting employee morale, and monetary savings. This project is expected to realize annual cost savings of more than $210,000."

■ Baxter Healthcare—Injection Site Process Management Team:

"This project team outlined improvements made to an assembly process that struggled to meet performance and quality measures. Problem-solving tools were utilized to identify the problem, understand variation, identify solutions, and implement final actions. Results verified improvements in all areas, including a 34 percent reduction in scrap and a 40 percent improvement in productivity."

- The Boeing Co.—The Ramp Team:

    "Quality, schedule, and cost problems plagued the flight ramp on the C-17 program. The Ramp Team examined itself and initiated improvement projects in five key areas: safety, people, processes, management, and facilities. The projects resulted in benchmark-level metric improvements, numerous national quality awards, and sixty additional airplane orders."

- Ethicon Endo-Surgery Inc., a Johnson & Johnson Co.—Sales Force Effectiveness:

    "Using Six Sigma methodology, this team used tools such as mapping, surveys, and statistical analyses to uncover the key drivers of performance among sales representatives. The resulting data helped this team determine that training and addressing specific selling skills would have a positive impact on sales revenue using minimal resources. Results are on track to exceed $15 million in incremental revenue by year end."

Here are some other typical examples:

- By redesigning its process, Federal Mogul was able to reduce its development process from twenty weeks to approximately twenty business days, resulting in a 75-percent reduction in throughput time.
- Prudential Insurance Co. focused on improving its processes and within eight months saw the following improvements:
    - ☐ Clerical errors down 90 percent
    - ☐ Productivity up 32 percent
    - ☐ Processing time down 20 percent

- One organization's delinquent accounts receivables had remained above $7 million for the past twelve months when a team attacked the process. The redesigned process improved cash flow and finance charges, saving more than $350,000 annually.
- When IBM looked at its accounting process, it found that overtime was running at 48 percent and miscodes were running at 2 percent. One million items were coded per day. As a result of redesigning the processes, overtime was reduced to less than 3 percent and miscodes dropped to less than 0.4 percent. In accounting most time is spent on correcting errors. When IBM started the process redesign effort, 62 percent of the accounting costs were poor quality cost.
- Stanford Hospital and Clinic focused upon improving its coronary artery bypass process. As a result of this team's activities:
    - ☐ Costs dropped by 40 percent
    - ☐ Mortality rate went down 3.9 percent
    - ☐ ICU time dropped by eight hours per patient

☐ Pulmonary artery catheter usage dropped by 15 percent
☐ Cumulated costs reduction totaled $15 million per year

Their process improvement activities in purchasing and other areas are saving the Stanford Hospital and Clinic another $25 million per year.

■ Excessive rejects at a glass manufacturing plant were caused by scratches and chips created by contamination in the process. By applying process improvement tools, rejects were reduced by 92 percent, line up-time improved 79 percent, and the organization realized a $840,000 per year savings.
■ Clients of a mutual fund company were unable to make informed decisions because asset values on the Web site did not have timely updates. Process improvement was applied, resulting in timely updates, retention of key clients, and a 20-percent reduction in operating costs.

Of course, there are hundreds of other examples of results organizations have obtained by focusing on process improvement, and many realized more significant improvement than in the preceding examples. By now you should have an idea of what you might expect when you focus on process improvement.

In "Six Sigma in Quality Programs," published in the spring 2003 issue of *Journal of Quality and Participation*, Robert Reid did a good job summarizing in a single figure the effect different process improvement methodologies have on the processes they are applied to. (See figure 8.1.)

Processes are vital to organizational excellence. Too often, management has taken away employees' ability to do error-free work because they haven't provided them with processes that are capable of performing error-free. The costs resulting from poor process man-

Figure 8.1 Examples of Process Improvement

Type characteristic	Status quo	Incremental	Design Redesign	Design Reengineering	Transformation	Revolution
Action	Change nothing	Solve Problems	Remove complexity	Create new process	Create different organization	Create new organization
Returns	0%	1–10%	10–50%	100–300%	200–500%	?
Success	100%	95%	80%	30%	10%	3%
Who	Everyone	Service provider	Middle management	Upper management	Executives	Leaders
Tools	Not needed	Statistical "many"	Process map "many"	Clean sheet of paper	Financial "many"	Formatted workspace

© 2003 American Society for Quality

agement can run as high as 75 percent of the total cost in departments such as research and development, accounting, and sales, and as much as 30 percent in manufacturing. Organizations that do a good job of process management reduce cost, cut cycle time, and improve customer satisfaction by providing reliable, high-quality output that customers can depend upon.

"Processes define how we operate. Projects are the way we improve our processes."

—HJH

APPENDIX A

DEFINITIONS

- **Activities**—small parts of a process usually performed by a single department or individual.
- **Affinity diagram**—a technique for organizing a variety of subjective data (such as options) into categories based on the intuitive relationships among individual pieces of information. Often used to find common points among concerns and ideas.
- **Arrow diagrams**—a way to define the most effective sequence of events and control the activity to meet a specific objective in a minimum amount of time. It is an adaptation of PERT (Program Evaluation and Review Technique) or the CPM (Critical Path Method).
- **Autonomous work team/self-managed work team**—a team approach that is used when a natural work team and the measurement system have developed to the point that employees can manage themselves. These teams select the improvement opportunities they will work on.
- **Brainstorming**—a technique used by a group to quickly generate large lists of ideas, problems, or issues. The emphasis is on quantity of ideas, not quality.
- **Bureaucracy elimination method**—an approach to identify and eliminate checks and balances activities that are not cost-justified.
- **Cause-and-effect diagram**—a visual presentation of possible causes of a specific problem or condition. The effect is listed on the right-hand side, and the causes take the shape of fish bones. It is sometimes called a fishbone diagram or Ishikawa diagram.
- **Certification**—a designed experiment applied to a single activity or piece of equipment. The item is considered certified when the evaluating team is confident that the individual activity, individual, or piece of equipment, when following the related procedures, will provide output that meets the next activity requirement.
- **Check sheet**—a simple form on which data are recorded in a uniform manner. The forms are used to minimize the risk of errors and facilitate the organized collection and analysis of data.
- **Control chart**—a tool that provides a picture of the way a process is performing. It is a graphical chart with control limits and plotted values. The values are a statistical measure for a series of samples or subgroups of the process output. A solid line shows the mean (average) of the output.

- **Delphi narrowing technique**—a technique by which team members' priorities are used to reduce a list of alternatives to a few of the most important alternatives.
- **Design of experiments**—structured evaluations designed to yield a maximum amount of information at a defined confidence level for the least expense. They are a set of principles and formulas for designing statistically sound evaluations.
- **Document control**—a process designed to remove obsolete documents from the operational area and ensure that only the correct level document is available to the employees. It includes document level controls.
- **Error-proofing**—designing the product and the processes so that it is very difficult for errors to occur.
- **Explicit knowledge**—knowledge that is stored in a semistructured medium such as documents, e-mail, voice mail, or video media. Often referred to as hard or tangible knowledge. It is conveyed from one person to another in a systematic way.
- **External customer**—an individual or organization that is not within the supplier's organization but receives a product, a service, or information from the supplier.
- **Failure mode and effects analysis**—identifies potential failures or causes of failures that might occur as a result of process design weaknesses.
- **Five Ss**—a system designed to bring organization to the workplace. A translation of the original five "S" terms from Japanese to English is:
  - □ *Seiri*—organization
  - □ *Seiton*—orderliness
  - □ *Seiso*—cleanliness
  - □ *Seiketsu*—standardized cleanup
  - □ *Shitsuke*—discipline

- **Five Ws and Two Hs**—a rigid, structured approach that probes into and defines a problem by asking a specific set of questions related to a previously defined opportunity or problem statement. The 5 Ws and 2 Hs stand for:
  - □ W1—What?
  - □ W2—Why?
  - □ W3—Where?
  - □ W4—Who?
  - □ W5—When?
  - □ H1—How did it happen?
  - □ H2—How much did it cost?

- **Flowchart**—a method of graphically describing a process (existing or proposed) by using simple symbols, lines, and words to display the sequence of activities in the process.

- **Force field analysis**—a visual aid for pinpointing and analyzing elements that resist change (restraining forces) or push for change (driving forces). This technique helps drive improvement by developing plans to overcome the restraining forces and make maximum use of the driving forces.
- **Function diagrams**—a systematic way of graphically displaying detailed tasks related to broader objectives or detailed issues related to broader issues.
- **Graphs**—visual displays of quantitative data that summarize a set of numbers or statistics.
- **Histogram**—a visual representation of the spread or distribution, using a series of rectangles (bars) of equal class sizes or widths. The heights of the bars indicate the relative number of data points in each class.
- **ISO 9000**—a set of standards released by the International Organization for Standardization that defines the fundamental building blocks for a quality management system and the associated accreditation and registration of quality management systems.
- **Internal customer**—a person, process, or department within an organization that receives output from another person and/or process within the same organization.
- **Interviewing techniques**—a structured discussion with one or more people for the purpose of collecting information related to a specific subject.
- **Interrelationship diagram**—a way to graphically map out the cause-and-effect links among related items.
- **Just-in-time**—a major strategy that allows an organization to produce only what is needed, when it's needed, to satisfy immediate customer requirements. Implemented effectively, the just-in-time concept will almost eliminate in-process stock.
- *Kaizen*—the Japanese word meaning "continuous improvement."
- **Knowledge**—a mixture of experiences, practices, traditions, values, contextual information, expert insight, and sound intuition that provides an environment and framework for evaluating and incorporating new experiences and information.
- **Knowledge management**—a proactive, systematic process by which value is generated from intellectual or knowledge-based assets and disseminated to the stakeholders.
- **Matrix diagram**—a systematic way of selecting from large lists of alternatives. They are used to choose between problems, root causes, or solutions. They are sometimes called decision matrices.
- **Milestone graph**—a graph that shows the goals or target to be achieved by depicting the projected schedule of the process. A primary purpose of this graph is to help organize projects and coordinate activities.
- **Mind map**—an unstructured cause-and-effect diagram. Also called a mind-flow or brain web.

- **Nominal group technique**—a technique useful for situations where individual judgments must be tapped and combined to arrive at decisions.

- **Organizational change management**—a methodology designed to lessen the stress and resistance of employees and management to individual critical changes. This is sometimes called managing organizational change.

- **Pareto diagram**—a type of chart in which the bars are arranged in descending order from the left to the right. It is a way to highlight "the vital few" in contrast to "the trivial many."

- **Poor quality cost**—a methodology that defines and collects costs related to resources (actual or potential) that are wasted or lost as a result of the organization's inability to do everything correctly every time. It includes both direct and indirect costs.

- **Process**—a series of logically interconnected, related activities that takes input, adds value to it, and produces output to an internal or external customer. It's how an organization's day-to-day routines work. An organization's processes define how it operates.

- **Process adaptability**—the flexibility of a process to handle future, changing customer expectations and today's individual, special customer requests. It is managing the process to meet today's special needs and future requirements. Adaptability is an area largely ignored but critical for gaining a competitive edge in the marketplace.

- **Process benchmarking**—a systematic way to identify superior processes and practices that are adopted for a process and then adapted to reduce cost, decrease cycle time, cut inventory, and provide greater satisfaction for internal and external customers.

- **Process capability studies**—a statistical comparison of a measurement pattern or distribution against specification limits to determine if a process can consistently deliver products within those limits.

- **Process decision program chart**—a method that maps out the events and contingencies that might occur when moving from an identified problem to one or more possible solutions.

- **Process effectiveness**—the extent to which the outputs of a process or subprocess meet the needs and expectations of its customers. This is a lot like quality but is more inclusive. Effectiveness is having the right output at the right place, at the right time, at the right price.

- **Process efficiency**—the extent to which resources are minimized and waste is eliminated in the pursuit of effectiveness. Productivity is a measure of efficiency.

- **Project**—a temporary endeavor undertaken to create a unique product or service.

- **Project management**—the application of knowledge, skills, tools, and techniques to project activities to meet or exceed stakeholders' needs and expectations from a project.

- **Qualification**—a designed experiment that involves evaluating a complex process consisting of many individual certified activities to determine whether the process can perform at an appropriate level when the activities are linked together. To be qualified, the process must demonstrate it can repeatedly deliver products and/or services on time, at the appropriate cost, and meet customer expectations on an ongoing basis.

- **Quality control circles**—teams made up mostly of volunteers, who hold short meetings over a definite period of time and work on either departmental or organizational problems that they select. As Yoshio Kondo, the founder of quality control circles, stated, "Quality control circles are to motivate employees, not to reduce costs."

- **Quality function deployment**—a structured process for taking the "voice of the customer," translating it into measurable customer requirements, translating the customer requirements into measurable counterpart characteristics, and deploying those requirements into every level of the product and manufacturing process design and all customer service processes.

- **Root cause analysis**—the process of identifying the various causes affecting a particular problem, process, or issue and determining the real reasons that caused the condition.

- **Run charts**—a graphic display of data used to assess the stability of a process over time or during a sequence of events (such as the number of batches produced). The run chart is the simplest form of control chart.

- **Scatter diagrams**—a graphic tool used to study the relationship between two variables. A scatter diagram is used to test for possible cause-and-effect relationships. It does not prove that one variable causes the other, but it does show whether a relationship exists and, if so, reveals the character of that relationship.

- **Shewhart cycle**—a structured approach for the improvement of services, products, and/or processes, developed by Walter Shewhart. Also known as the plan-do-check-act cycle.

- **Simulation modeling**—using computer programs to represent the item (e.g., activity, process, or system) under study to predict how it will perform or to control its performance.

- **Six Sigma program**—a program designed to reduce error rates to a maximum of 3.44 errors per million units, developed by Motorola during the late 1980s.

- **Statistical process control**—using data for controlling processes; making outputs of products or services predictable. A mathematical approach to understanding and managing activities. It includes three statistical quality tools: design of experiments, control charts, and characterization.

- **Suggestion system**—a system that asks employees to document their ideas and hand them into management, which assigns them to someone for investigation and implementation if acceptable. Usually the employee(s) who turned in the idea shares the money the organization gets from implementing the idea. The suggestion approach was started by National Cash Register in 1896.

- **Supplier qualification**—the act of evaluating a supplier to determine if it has an adequate management system to ensure there is a high probability that it will provide an output that meets requirements.
- **System**—groups of related processes that might or might not be connected.
- **Tacit knowledge**—knowledge that is formed around intangible factors embedded in an individual's experience. This is personal, content-specific knowledge that resides in an individual. It is knowledge that an individual gains from experience or skills that he or she develops. It often takes the form of beliefs, values, principles, and morals. It guides the individual's actions. It is referred to as "soft" knowledge. It is embedded in the individual's ideas, insights, values, and judgment. It is only accessible through direct corroboration and communication with the individual who has the knowledge.
- **Tasks**—steps that are required to perform a specific activity
- **Task forces**—these teams are used when a major improvement opportunity that must be reacted to immediately is identified by management.
- **Task teams**—these teams are used when management identifies an improvement opportunity and assigns employees to solve it.
- **Tree diagram**—a systematic approach that helps the user think about each phase or aspect of solving a problem, reaching a target, or achieving a goal.
- **Value-added analysis**—a procedure for analyzing every activity within a process, classifying it as value-adding or nonvalue-adding, and then taking positive action to eliminate, or at least minimize, the nonvalue-adding activities or tasks.

APPENDIX B

TYPICAL BUSINESS PROCESSES

Function	Process Name
Development	Records management
	Acoustics control design
	Advanced communication development
	Cable component design
	Reliability management
	Cost target
	Design test
	Design/material review
	Document review
	High-level design specification
	Industrial design
	Inter-divisional liaison
	Logic design and verification
	Component qualification
	Power system design
	Product management
	Product publication
	Release
	System-level product design
	System reliability and serviceability
	System requirements
	Tool design
	User/system interface design
	Competitive analysis
	Design systems support
	Engineering operations
	Information development
	Interconnect planning

Interconnect product development
Physical design tools
Systems design
Engineering change management
Product development
Tool development
Development process control
Electronic development
Phase 0/requirement

Distribution

Receiving
Shipping
Storage
Field services/support
Teleprocessing and control
Parts expediting
Power vehicles
Salvage
Transportation
Production receipts
Disbursement
Inventory management
Physical inventory management

Financial accounting

Ledger control
Financial control
Payroll
Taxes
Transfer pricing
Accounts receivable
Accrual accounting
Revenue accounting
Accounts payable
Cash control
Employee expense account
Fixed asset control
Labor distribution
Cost accounting
Financial application

	Fixed assets/appropriation
	Intercompany accounting/billing
	Inventory control
	Procurement support
	Financial control

Financial planning   Appropriation control
Budget control
Cost estimating
Financial planning
Transfer pricing
Inventory control
Business planning
Contract management
Financial outlook

Information systems   Applications development methodology
Systems management controls
Service-level assessment

Production control   Consignment process
Customer order services management
Early manufacturing involvement and product release
EC implementation
Field parts support
Parts planning and ordering
Planning and scheduling management
Plant business volumes performance management
Site-sensitive parts
Systems WIP management
Allocation
Inventory projection
New product planning
WIP accuracy
Base plan commit
Manufacturing process record

Purchasing   Alteration/cancellation
Expediting
Invoice/payment
Supplier selection
Cost
Delivery
Quality
Supplier relations
Contracts
Lab procurement
Nonproduction orders
Production orders
Supplier payment
Process interplant transfer

Personnel   Benefits
Compensation
Employee relations
Employment
Equal opportunity
Executive resources
Management development
Medical
Personnel research
Personnel services
Placement
Records
Suggestions
Management development/research
Personnel programs
Personnel assessment
Resource management

Programming   Distributed systems products
Programming center
Software development
Software engineering
Software manufacturing products

Quality   New products qualification
                     Supplier quality

Site services   Facilities change request

Miscellaneous   Cost of box manufacturing quality
                     Service cost estimating
                     Site planning

APPENDIX C

IBM'S PROCESS QUALIFICATION PROCEDURE

As the model process converts over to a production process, the process continues to expand, adding additional equipment to the manufacturing facility. Hard tooling replaces soft tooling, and automation moves into manufacturing. During this growth period, sufficient quantities of products are being produced to allow extremes of specifications, equipment settings, and vended materials to be evaluated by process capability studies.

THE PURPOSES OF PROCESS QUALIFICATION

- Characterize the process as it undergoes scale-up and automation.
- Develop and refine control procedures.
- Ensure the continuation of a customer-shippable product.
- Provide management with yield and manufacturability assessments.
- Measure the outgoing quality levels of the process.
- Define first-customer ship product level.

THE THREE PARTS OF PROCESS QUALIFICATION

1. Process Certification
- Certifying that the critical operation can produce a high-quality product to specification when the expected process variation is taken into consideration
- Evaluating the process to ensure that planned production improvements meet first-customer ship requirements
- Comparing of actual yield to planned yield

2. Qualification Lots
- Qualification lots are produced to measure the product performance at installation and compare it to committed performance. This includes a mixture of field-replaceable units and products installed in ship-level hardware. This evaluation is conducted in the quality assurance product measurement analysis laboratory.

3. Technical Exposures

■ Evaluation of technical exposures that could effect manufacturability, quality, or field performance.

THE REQUIREMENTS FOR PROCESS CERTIFICATION

The prerequisites to begin process certification are:

Documentation

■ Engineering documentation

■ Software documentation

■ Maintenance procedures

■ Quality program plan

☐ By this time, the quality program plan should be completed and all scheduled commitments met.

■ All quality assurance documentation released

☐ Inspection instructions and audit plans must have successfully completed a review by manufacturing, manufacturing engineering, and development engineering and be formally released to the manufacturing floor. This includes in-process audits and gate inspections as well as receiving inspection instructions.

■ All development engineering documents must be released to manufacturing.

☐ This means that all prints, specifications, and performance specifications must have successfully completed a review by manufacturing engineering, quality engineering, and production control and be formally released through the document control center.

■ All manufacturing documentation released

☐ This means that all manufacturing process instructions, tester operating instructions, tester calibration instructions, chemical purchase requirements, manufacturing routings, and traveler cards must have completed a successful review by manufacturing, quality assurance, and development engineering, and been formally released.

■ Test equipment and tooling prints must be complete

☐ Complete documentation of the test equipment and tooling drawings must be available for quality assurance to complete the certification. A control system must be maintained over print change levels so that future certifications can take advantage of past information.

- Workmanship standards must by available
  - □ In many cases, due to the complexity of verbally defining the difference between acceptable and unacceptable, engineering documentation must be supplemented by visual workmanship standards when visual inspection operations are involved.

- Outgoing quality levels
  - □ An agreed-upon, outgoing quality level must be signed off by sending and receiving, manufacturing, quality assurance, and development engineering groups. In addition, the installation and early-life performance must be agreed to by manufacturing, quality assurance, development engineering, and customer engineering. In both cases, quality assurance is responsible for developing a document of understanding that is approved by the aforementioned functions.

- Stress tests to ensure manufacturing product reliability
  - □ By this point in the program, development engineering should have released documentation defining any continuing stress tests that need to be performed by quality assurance to ensure continuing product reliability. Typical stress tests include temperature, shock, vibration, impact shock, humidity, corrosion, and start/stop wear.

- Process compatibility plan
  - □ When multiple plants will be manufacturing the same product, process capability is a corporate requirement between locations. Process compatibility entails:
    - Optimizing process commonality
    - Identifying and controlling differences for the purpose of achieving product and subproduct interchangeability in terms of quality, function, reliability, and physical interface on a worldwide basis.

  - □ Quality assurance heads a team that is responsible for developing a plan that will ensure process compatibility. This plan includes an operation-by-operation comparison of the two manufacturing processes, a parts exchange program, and an equipment correlation program.

- Rework procedure
  - □ No rework operation can be performed on the line unless rework routing, manufacturing process instructions and traveler cards are released, accompanied by adequate manufacturing training documentation. The quality engineer should evaluate the

adequacy of these documents, obtain copies of each after they have completed the four-way sign-off cycle, and add them to his or her history file.

Test/Process Equipment

- Equipment accepted by maintenance
  - ☐ At this point in time, maintenance should have assumed responsibility for maintaining all process equipment. Exceptions to this will require a detailed plan explaining the schedule leading up to maintenance acceptance of the equipment and an explanation why the equipment has not been accepted by maintenance.

- Long-term precision drift evaluations completed
  - ☐ Calibration schedules are based on long-term equipment drift evaluation. Drift evaluations should be completed so that calibration schedules can be assessed for correctness. This requires that a monitoring program be implemented on critical process equipment during this period.

- Extremes of settings evaluated
  - ☐ This evaluation includes two variables: the variation in settings allowed in the equipment and the variation of the product submitted to the equipment. Before certification is granted, critical equipment will be evaluated to determine how well it performs when set at the extremes of the equipment settings, as specified in the manufacturing process instruction and calibration instruction. In addition, the equipment will be evaluated while processing product that is at the extremes of the engineering specification. These evaluations are conducted to determine the safety factor designed into the product and the equipment, and the effects of these variations on yield.

- Manufacturing training program implemented
  - ☐ The effectiveness of manufacturing's training program to prepare a new operator to produce customer-shippable products will be evaluated and discrepancies in the program corrected.

- Equipment certification/correlation
  - ☐ As the process expands, additional test inspection and manufacturing equipment comes on line. It is imperative that this equipment be certified by quality assurance, and correlation studies be conducted between pieces of equipment to ensure that accept/reject criteria for each piece of equipment is the same. Correlation studies are normally performed using marginal hardware as accepted or rejected from the primary piece of equipment. These same correlation studies must be performed between the primary and remote locations to ensure parts interchangeability.

Processes

■ Process capabilities studies completed

  ☐ Selected critical operations will have process capabilities studies performed on them. The purpose of these studies is to evaluate and establish limits for the equipment under ideal conditions. These limits can then be applied to an individual application to ensure that the equipment is not used in an application that it can't perform repeatedly.

■ Process variation analysis completed

  ☐ With the increase in production materials, products can be selected at the extremes of the engineering specification and the manufacturing distribution. Using these selected parts, design experiments are conducted to determine the safety factor in the engineering design. Often these experiments identify processes that need to be improved and/or engineering specifications that can be relaxed.

■ Process controls completely implemented

  ☐ As you prepare to meet the high production period just before and after first customer ship, it is imperative that the quality program takes on a new dimension. Emphasis must shift from the parts acceptance mode to a process controls mode, where the variables that affect the process are controlled, thereby ensuring the product produced meets the quality and reliability requirements. One of the ways to accomplish this is by the use of control charts. Control charts are used to predict outcome and to correct trends before they become problems. To determine what affects product quality and reliability and where and how these efforts can be controlled, a cause-and-effect analysis must be conducted for defects detected during the evaluation period. Of course, many of the control points are also identified during the program's design review cycle. (For individual operations whose Cpk is less than 1.4, sorting operations must be established.)

■ Quality assurance in-process audit inspection and control program completely implemented

  ☐ As the process control concept is implemented, it is necessary to change the inspector's role. This means the inspector will spend less time doing gate inspection operations and more time doing audits and collecting control data. Typical audits that will be conducted are operator, calibration, scrap, documentation, storage, process flow, maintenance, chemical, and storage life. In addition, the inspector will be the source of much of the variables data that are needed to maintain the control charts located throughout the process.

  ☐ Quality reporting system implemented

☐ For the process to be certified, the quality reporting system must be working effectively. This means that defect and yield reports are generated on a regular basis and reported back to manufacturing. This program should include some visual means of communicating to the manufacturing employee the quality of the work being produced in his or her area (e.g., quality graphs posted in the work area). It should also include an operator quality report for the manufacturing managers that provides information about the quality of the work being produced by each of their operators.

■ Process compatibility assessment completed

☐ When process-sensitive products are multisourced, it becomes difficult to achieve process compatibility on a worldwide basis without a high degree of interchange between plants. Process compatibility between plants producing the same product should be the objective of all high-technology processes where the product can't be specified independently of the process that produces it. To accomplish this, a comprehensive process compatibility program must be established.

Product

■ Process yields

☐ The product should be progressing along the yield improvement curves committed to in the last phase estimate.

■ Process quality

☐ The product should reach an acceptable quality level at each point in the manufacturing cycle, as measured by the quality gates and audit activities. When a quality measurement point falls below target, an aggressive corrective action plan must be prepared to bring the condition back under control.

■ First customer-ship-performance target levels as measured in the machine and as field-replaceable units

☐ These evaluations are conducted in the product measurement analysis lab at this system's level. A document of understanding is prepared when quality assurance, manufacturing, test engineering, product engineering, and field engineering agree to sample size and a performance criteria based upon the tests that will be conducted in the product measurement analysis lab.

■ Reliability/environmental requirements

☐ Reliability/environmental testing is performed in the product measurement analysis laboratory and in the product assurance laboratory to determine susceptibility of the product to environmental extremes and to predict product reliability.

- Committed outgoing quality levels
    - ☐ The product should be meeting all committed outgoing quality levels. This means that the components and subassemblies should not be exceeding committed return rates from the higher-level assemblies.

Qualification Lot

The purpose of these qualification lots is to measure the ship quality level of the component both in the machine and at the FRU ship level. Requirements for this evaluation are:

- An agreed-upon installation and early-life target for the component
- An agreed-upon qualification lot plan. This plan specifies the sample size, the tests that will be performed, and expected acceptable levels of performance to provide a high level of confidence that the product shipped to the first customer, and all following customers, will meet the initial early-life performance targets.
- The evaluation is conducted at the systems level and stimulates customers' application
- Components will be representative of the first customer-ship hardware and engineering change level
- All failures that occur during this test will undergo a comprehensive failure analysis evaluation, and corrective action will be taken to eliminate the problem's recurrence.

Failure to successfully complete this evaluation means the defined process is unable to meet its first-customer ship requirements and that the process must be upgraded to improve field performance before it will be supported by quality assurance for shipment to customers.

These process modifications normally are divided into two separate activities:

- Changes that cause the defect to be screened out in-plant. Typical screening activities would be:
    - ☐ Component burn-in
    - ☐ System-level testing on all components
    - ☐ Longer and more stringent unit and/or component tests

- Changes that prevent the problem from occurring. These changes require modifications to the basic process and/or engineering design. This type of preventive action usually requires more time to implement because it involves changes to equipment, fixtures, and/or materials.

Both of these activities are usually required. The first is necessary to ensure that the product shipped meets customer expectations and provides a screening mechanism until the preventive action can be implemented and components are cycled through the new process. The second action is necessary so that the expensive, unplanned screening operations can be eliminated and cost objectives met.

Regression Analysis

When the qualification lot starts through the manufacturing cycle, after the completion of ship verification test, a regression analysis will be performed comparing the process and product to the process and product that the engineering release was based upon. There must be no degradation in either the process or product quality.

Resolution of All Major Technical Exposures

- Independent audit
  - ☐ A group of process specialists from other programs must perform an independent audit on the quality and manufacturing programs that support the process. The audit team will normally consist of representatives from quality assurance, product engineering, and manufacturing engineering. The results of this audit will be completely documented, and corrective action programs must be completed before the process is qualified.

- Process technical exposures
  - ☐ At this time, there should be no outstanding issues related to product performance, process variation, manufacturability assessment, and process stability.

INDEX